What people say:

'A highly effective trainer, coach, and assessor who strives for excellence in everything she does. Her knowledge of work-based learning and adult education is outstanding and she offers good support to those she teaches and mentors, particularly through drawing on her own personal experience as an adult learner.'

Andrew Ellams, MD Ellams Associates Ltd.

'An inspirational individual and dedicated professional who gives and shares only her best. She's been very thoughtful and creative in her visionary approach to support the education sector, strengthen stakeholder relationships and guiding individuals to achieve their aspirations and goals.'

Prabhjit Kaur—PGCE(FE,) CMgr MCMI, AssocCIPD, MBA(Open) PGCE(FE).

'A detailed and passionate professional, who loves to share her knowledge with anyone who will listen.'

Joanna Kinch, MD Kinch Print Ltd.

About the Author

Rosalie Marsh is an award-winning author and a native of Lancashire with Irish roots.

Today she lives in North Wales where she settled with her husband and growing family. Rosalie has written many academic, vocational, technical and research materials in her long and varied career in banking, sales management, and further education. It was during this latter period that she gained a BA (Hons) Education Degree from the Manchester Metropolitan University.

Rosalie retired to concentrate on her writing. Her first book *Just Us Two: Ned and Rosie's Gold Wing Discovery*, Winner in the 2010 International Book Awards (Travel: Recreational category), was also a UK bestseller and finalist in the USA Book News 2009 Best Books Awards. Her Lifelong Learning: Personal Effectiveness Guides build on her wide experience in the workplace along with adult and further education in the field of work-based learning.

Rosalie embraces new technologies and digital solutions. Her books therefore are always available in print and e-book formats. Rosalie writes under a pen name.

Connect with Rosalie at:
http://www.discover-rosalie.com
http://www.discover-rosalie.blogspot.com

Also by Rosalie Marsh

Just Us Two Travel Series.

Just Us Two: Ned and Rosie's Gold Wing Discovery.
Winner 2010 International Book Awards (Travel: Recreational).
Chasing Rainbows: with Just Us Two.

Lifelong Learning: Personal Effectiveness Guides.

Lifelong Learning: A View from the Coalface.
Release Your Potential: Making Sense of Personal and Professional Development.
Skills for Employability Part One: Pre-Employment.
Skills for Employability Part Two: Moving into Employment. (November 2012)

Future Releases.

Island Interludes: Just Us Two Escape to the Sun.
The Long Leg of Italy: Just Us Two Explore the Diversity of Italy.
Talking the Talk: Getting the Message Across.
Customer? What Customer? Some Basic Essentials in Customer Service.

Skills

for

Employability

Part One

by
Rosalie Marsh

C

Christal Publishing

CHRISTAL PUBLISHING
11, Briarswood, Rhosrobin, WREXHAM LL11 4PX
www.christalpublishing.com

Cover Design ©Christal Publishing
www.discover-rosalie.com

First published 2012 by Christal Publishing.
ISBN 978-1-908302-16-8 Perfect Bound Soft Cover.
ISBN 978-1-908302-17-5 e-book-Kindle.
ISBN 978-1-908302-18-2 e-book-Adobe DRM.
ISBN 978-1-908302-19-9 e-book-ePub.

British Library Cataloguing in Publication Data. A catalogue record for this book is available from the British Library.

This book is printed on environmentally friendly paper from responsible sources.

Microsoft® product screen shots reprinted with permission from Microsoft Corporation. Microsoft, Encarta, MSN, and Windows are either registered trademarks or trademarks of Microsoft Corporation in the United States and/or other countries.

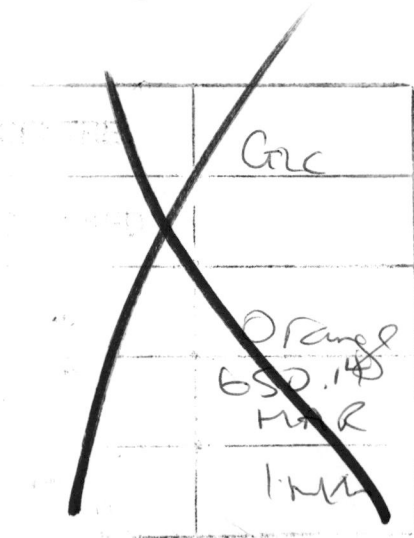

Contents

Foreword 1

Features and Benefits 3

Overview of *Skills for Employability Part One.* 7

Chapter One. Preparing for Work. 11

Chapter Two. Job Applications. 23

Chapter Three. Working Effectively in the Workplace. .. 43

Chapter Four. ICT Skills in the Workplace. 73

Progression. Where do I go from here? 113

Useful Links and Resources 115

Further Reading.

Foreword

The target audience for this book is diverse. This includes those at pre-employment stage e.g. school leavers up to graduates; 16-18 year old unemployed who have not obtained sufficient grades to follow their preferred path; returners to work; those with disabilities who are seeking a change of employment; those in employment and seeking to enhance their prospects or are between jobs. Currently [01.2012] there are over 1 million people in the UK who are 'Not in Employment, Education, or Training' (NEETS).

Many do not have the life skills and/or a basic understanding of what is required to become and stay employed and enhance their future. This book—one of a series—will provide essential information to fill the gaps identified through research and enhance the prospects of a successful interview.

There are many publications which address the gaps in adult literacy, numeracy, and Key Stage 4. The whole raft of knowledge needed for employability and personal development—on which business success depends—is not currently fully represented. This book will address those aspects of employability relating to current business and work-related practice. Currently, most practitioners engaged in work-based learning design and develop their own training programmes. This book will reduce the burden. It is designed to be a non-threatening user-friendly resource for anyone to use whether or not they attend a formal training course.

Those seeking employment may be familiar with much of what is normally (but often not) contained in an induction programme. This book will enhance the process; learners will be entering employment forearmed; it will be a reference in the future.

Much of the content is embedded in the mandatory units of various vocational qualifications. The chapters are signposted to units accredited in the QCF including SSA Units 14.1 Foundations for Learning and Life and 14.2 Preparation for Work; OCR Personal Life Skills; OCR Employability Skills; City and Guilds Employability and Personal Development (7546) Units. The knowledge in this book could be presented for accreditation of prior learning and therefore speed up achievement for the learner.

Author Note:

'Essential Skills Wales (ESW) are the fundamental qualifications for reading, writing, maths and IT in Wales. They're designed to help you apply your skills to real situations—from adding up bills to creating a CV. You can get a qualification in three skill areas—Communication, Application of Number and Information and Communication Technology (ICT).'
http://www.cityandguilds.com/57650.html?s=1 03.02.2012

'In Wales, the accreditation end date for Wider Key Skills has been extended to August 2014. The Wider Key Skills standards are currently being revised and it is anticipated that the revised qualifications will become part of the Essential Skills Wales suite from September 2012.'
http://www.ocr.org.uk/qualifications/type/esw/ 03.02.2012.

Therefore, in the interests of inclusiveness, the topics are signposted—where relevant—to Functional Skills, Essential Skills Wales—Communication, Application of Number, Information Communication Technology [ICT]—, and the Wider Key Skills Working with Others, Improving Own Learning and Performance and Problem Solving.

Features and Benefits

For those seeking employment:

Features.

➢ Each chapter/section will detail the learning outcomes and relevance to other qualifications.

➢ At the end of each topic, there will be a series of questions/activities for self-assessment to check learner progress. In turn, this will add to a sense of achievement.

➢ Learners will be able to measure how far they have travelled.

➢ Much of the content will feed into and is signposted to Functional Skills; Awards and Certificates in Employability and Personal Development; or Personal Life and Employability Skills, all of which are linked to the Qualification Credit Framework (QCF).

➢ All content will relate to the current gaps in knowledge & understanding and softer skills for those who are pre-employment e.g. Year 10 and Year-11 school leavers; 16-18 year old unemployed; returners to work; learners with disabilities who are seeking a change of employment, are in employment and seeking to enhance their prospects or are between jobs.

➢ The book will have some illustrations to enhance text.

➢ There are links to websites e.g. for legislation and further current information. This will provide more interaction and variety for the learner and ensure currency of information.

Adult Literacy and Numeracy will not be addressed in this book, as there are many excellent resources available.

Benefits.

After completing Skills for Employability Part One: Pre-Employment, learners will:

➢ Have more awareness of the standards of behaviour and requirements of employers.

➢ Be introduced to health and safety in the workplace.

➢ Have an awareness of health, safety, and security relating to ICT in the workplace.

➢ Have completed short practical activities that aim to test their understanding.

➢ Have raised their self-esteem and confidence.

➢ Have an awareness and understanding of the business environment.

➢ Have some basic knowledge and understanding, which will feed into Awards/Certificates in Employability and Personal Life Skills/Development, vocational qualifications, or company training programmes.

For Teachers, Tutors, and Trainers:

Feature.

Available in print and e-book formats for most readers.

Benefit.

Time and cost savings. A ready-made resource reduces time and cost of design and/or photocopying.

Feature.

In print form, Skills for Employability Part One can be used in the traditional way with everyone having their own copy.

Benefits.

It can be taken away by the learner to be absorbed as part of homework or an assignment.

It can be issued as a resource for the course to be used as intended—as a workbook.

Feature

Available in a variety of e-book formats worldwide:

- Kindle and Kindle Apps for desktop, iBook, Android etc.
- Adobe Digital Editions DRM *pdf for desktop and readers for download from e-retailers worldwide.
- E-Pub. Apple iBookstore, Sony eBooks, Nook, Diesel eBooks, Kobo, Smashwords, and Blio.

Benefits.

- Can be downloaded to a PC and be tutor led via presentation screen or whiteboard with learners following from the print version.

- Can be downloaded to college computers or a hand-held reader for full interaction with tutors and learners.

- Cost effective. Budget will go further.

- Learners can adjust the font size and background colour to suit individual sight preferences, thus overcoming one of the barriers to reading enjoyment.

- The majority of learners are used to technology and reading on-screen.

- User-friendly.

Overview of
Skills for Employability Part One

Well Done! By opening this book, you have taken the first step to increasing your skills and knowledge to develop yourself, make you more employable, and enhance your future.

You may be on the verge of leaving school and looking for employment. Or you may have completed a course of study following leaving school or not worked at all. On the other hand, you may be in employment and are looking to better yourself and achieve those goals that you have only previously dreamed of achieving. The aim of this book is to fill any gaps in skills or knowledge and understanding you may have which prevent you from gaining employment or progressing in your current or future employment. It will prepare you for the world of work beyond your present horizons and set you on the road to achieve your full potential.

As already explained, the topics relate closely to other learning programmes. Learning here is flexible and completed in bite-size chunks where you can build 'stepping stones' to the future. Depending on 'where you are at' you can take as little or as much as you need from the learning experience.

The topics in this book also relate very closely to some of those skills that are an essential part of being employable. These are called Functional Skills.

What are Functional Skills?

Functional Skills describe different areas of skills and knowledge, which underpin effective performance in everyday life, both work and leisure. They are needed for continued employability and prosperity. They are a means of proving that you are working at the level needed in key areas of competence for your job role, and have often been underdeveloped and unrecognised in the past. Tasks you complete in one functional skill area often provide evidence for another.

> *'Functional Skills are the fundamental applied skills in English, Information and Communication Technology (ICT) and Mathematics—or Number— that help people to gain the most from life, learning and work. The skills are learning tools that enable people: to apply their knowledge and understanding to everyday life, to engage competently and confidently with others, to solve problems in both familiar and unfamiliar situations, to develop personally and professionally as positive citizens who can actively contribute to society.'* (Source Ofqual /09/4558)

To put it a little clearer, you need to be able to read and understand instructions and information, write clearly and spell correctly so that you are understood, and to be able to speak clearly and take part in conversations and discussions with people you work with.

You need to know how to handle numbers in everyday situations such as shopping, working out your wages to make sure you have been paid correctly, working out how much you will need to fill your car with petrol etc. So by mathematics, (do not freeze and hold up your hands in horror when you hear the word!) we really mean using numbers in all sorts of everyday situations at work, at home and in leisure.

Most organisations use computers—we are in a technological age. You will probably have used computers in school. If you have a computer at home, you will possibly have been able to widen your skills. However, there are still many homes without a computer or it is used mainly for surfing the Internet and playing games. It may be that your parents control the computer and you have not been allowed to use the various software packages such as Microsoft® Word or Microsoft® Works for letters and CV's, or simple spreadsheets for planning your budget or holiday.

You may have a job where you just use the system and are not involved in actually putting information onto the system. That is OK but you do need to be familiar with a computer and the keyboard and be competent at a basic level if you are going to increase your employability. If you work in an office *of any kind,* you will need good ICT skills.

So working with other people, improving your skills and standard of working and being able to work through and solve the kind of problems which crop up, are all achieved by having good levels of English, Mathematics (number) and computer skills. They underpin everything. Your employer, training provider and/or local college should have more information on these and the award and certificate above.

NB. Functional Skills are available in England and Northern Ireland.
Wales has its own policy and has developed Essential Skills Wales.'
http://wales.gov.uk/topics/educationandskills/learningproviders/
essentialskillswales/

Skills for Employability Part One: Pre-Employment is made up of chapters, which cover a number of topics.

Preparing for Work covers: identifying what employers are looking for, looking at job vacancies, identifying personal skills and qualities, a self assessment checklist, ,what do I need to do better/learn? Check your knowledge & Signposting to QCF Units.

Job Applications covers: writing a CV and covering letter, how to structure a CV., Pen Picture & strengths/weaknesses, going for an interview. Check your knowledge & Signposting to QCF Units.

Working Effectively in the Workplace covers: attitude and behaviour, getting to work, effective communication, working effectively. Check your knowledge. Signposting to QCF Units.

ICT Skills in the Workplace covers a self-assessment checklist of ICT skills, e-mail, Internet, health, safety, and security relating to ICT. Check your knowledge. Signposting to QCF Units.

Progression. Where do I go from here points you to the next stage of your journey.

Each chapter will detail the learning outcome (tell you what you will be learning). There will be a series of tasks for you to complete along the way as well as some links to the Internet where you can explore the topics in more detail. This is to give you some variety in your learning journey and to check your progress. In turn, you will have a sense of achievement and will be able to see how far you have travelled.

At the end of each chapter, there will be signposting to personal life development/employability awards and certificates, and/or Functional Skills. So if you read the topics carefully and complete all the tasks you could have some evidence to go towards this. This is called Accreditation of Prior Learning. No learning is ever wasted; learning can come from all sorts of situations both formal and informal, from work or from leisure activities. Once you have learned something, there is no need to go through the process again if it appears in a different qualification. Although this book is not designed to give you a qualification in itself—more to help you develop yourself—the bite-sized chunks mentioned in the Personal Life/Development and Employability Skills qualifications are given a credit value and are transferable. This book will contribute to the knowledge and understanding needed whether or not you are undertaking the qualification at this time.

Please turn now to Chapter One and begin your journey.

Chapter One.Preparing for Work

In this chapter we will start the ball rolling with trying to identify what employers are looking for. You not only have to find out what they are looking for in you as a person but also what kind of jobs are on offer.

Then we will look at a list of personal skills and qualities and identify what you already have. This will naturally lead on to identifying what you need to do better or learn.

At the end of this chapter you should be better prepared to apply for jobs and present yourself in a way to make an employer want to know more about you and invite you for an interview.

Identifying what employers are looking for: looking at job vacancies.

Wherever you are at in the job market, it is a good idea to find out just what employers have on offer. Of course, you may harbour dreams of sailing around the world or working in an obscure occupation. That is excellent. We all have dreams. However, the main thing is to find a job that is going to pay the mortgage or rent and put food on the table. We all have to start somewhere. Sometimes you have to take a step sideways, or even down, in order to move forward.

Local, Regional and National Press.

Don't just look at your usual local paper and leave it at that.

Try a selection of newspapers, which cover a larger area than your town. Another tip is to try one of the job-related newspapers, which come out every week and cover either a specific area or the whole country. These are usually divided up into various classified areas or types of jobs.

Job Centres.

If you need to talk to someone in person, you can find where your local job centre is located, in the telephone directory or at http://www.jobseekers.direct.gov.uk

On-line.

There is a lot of advice at specialist sites on the Internet.

Try http://www.direct.gov.uk/en/Employment/Jobseekers/Loo kingForWork/DG_10030134

On this site, there are many links with useful information about jobs all over the UK. There is also lots of useful information about applying for jobs and various volunteer programmes. If you have been out of work for a while, these actually are useful in giving you some experience of the world of work or getting you out among people. Not only will you show that you are willing to work; you might find that an opportunity of paid work opens up.

http://www.totaljobs.com/Content/Jobseeking_plus/Job-centres.html

On this site is a wealth of information where you can look at what types of jobs are on offer, what they pay, what the duties are and, more importantly, what skills and abilities you need.

Follow these links or try your own Internet search. *(Chapter Four of this book will help you here if you are not sure how to do this.)* Once you have identified what employers are looking for you will need to look at what you as a person can offer. You need to be sure that you as a person will fit that job role.

If you are looking to earn while you learn.

OK! So you have had enough of 'learning' you think to yourself. You want to get out there and earn some real money. To do that you need some skills, which unfortunately means carrying on learning. This however, does not need to be in an academic way. There are many routes to learning and gaining the knowledge for you to do what you really want to do.

An apprenticeship is another route into employment and learning valuable skills. Give this some thought. They are not just for school leavers. You learn alongside skilled people while doing things you enjoy.

'There may be different entry requirements depending on the Apprenticeship and the industry sector. However, competition for places with employers can be fierce, so you will need to show that you are committed, and aware of your responsibilities to both yourself and the company who would employ you. You also need to be happy to work as both part of a team and individually, and be able to use your own initiative.'
(Source:http://www.apprenticeships.org.uk/Be-An-Apprentice/The-Basics.aspx—Sourced:03.02.2012)
Visit this website for more information.

Local Information.

Sometimes, you know, you can find an interesting job advertised in a shop window or the post office. I once had a change of career when I saw an advert in local shop window advertising for a manager. I switched from direct sales to retail management and changed the whole course of my life.

Word of mouth is another source of information. So, keep your ear to the ground. It is important to be open-minded and flexible in your search. You never know what is around the corner and it is easier to get a job from a job even though you might not, at the moment, be doing what you dream of doing.

Be realistic in your expectations.

Self-employment.

It doesn't have to take a lot of money to set up in business. It depends on what you want to do. What you plan to do may involve working from home in a variety of situations. There is a wealth of information on the Government Direct.gov website. Just follow the links and see what you can find at http://www.direct.gov.uk/en/Employment/Jobseekers/Loo kingForWork/DG_173931

Voluntary work.

Your first thought on reaching this topic may be:

'Why should I work for nothing!'

Many times, you may be overlooked for a job because you lack experience. You can't get experience if you haven't got a job. It is a 'chicken and egg' situation. *(Which came first— the chicken or the egg?)*

Below is an excerpt from the direct.gov website, which puts it into focus.

'There are many benefits of volunteering. It is a great way of getting into a working environment, which could help you:

- *Develop new skills.*

- *Gain experience.*

- *Get training in new areas of work.*

- *Explore career interests.*

- *Increase your contacts, which could provide job leads.*

- *Build your confidence.*

- *Develop and enhance your CV.*

Volunteering is also a great way to support your community and can make a big difference locally.'

(http://www.direct.gov.uk/en/Employment/Jobseekers/LookingForWork/DG_10 033053. sourced 03.02.2012)

In addition, you will retain your self-respect and show that you are willing to work. Always an asset.

Identifying personal skills and qualities.

OK. You have looked at the types of jobs on offer.

Did any of them look appealing? Could you fill any of the vacancies? Make some notes.

You are going to have to convince a prospective employer that 'you are the one'. You will need to sell your qualities and suitability. You will need to convince your prospective employer that you will be an asset to the company.

Task:

Complete the following checklists to identify what skills and qualities you already have.

(Extracted from *Release Your Potential: Making Sense of Personal and Professional Development.* 2011.)

Personal Skills	Can do	Can do with help	This is difficult
Work on my own.			
Work with other people as part of a team.			
Thank people for their help.			
Organise and prioritise tasks.			
Keep a check on progress of tasks.			
Ask for help if I have a problem.			
Apologise if I am wrong.			
Accept feedback.			
Express my views clearly, and calmly.			
Listen to and respect other people's views.			
Think about a task before rushing in to start it.			
Good time keeping.			
If I am late or sick I telephone ahead.			
Respect other people.			
I am polite, helpful, and flexible.			
I am always clean and tidy in my dress.			

Work Skills	Can do	Can do with help	This is difficult
I make notes when I am researching for information.			
Discuss my work.			
Write about myself clearly.			
Take part in discussions and listen to other views.			
I know how to find information from different sources.			
Use a telephone.			
Accept responsibility.			
Keep to a timescale for tasks.			
Respond to challenges.			
Put away documents/papers/ equipment neatly & quickly.			
Persevere when things get difficult.			
Follow health & safety rules.			
Use a computer.			
Receive and send e-mails.			
Use word processing software.			
Can do simple mental calculations.			
Know how to use images in documents.			
Check my work for accuracy.			

What do I need to do better/learn?

In the next chapter, you will be learning how to set out your Curriculum Vitae, or CV, as they are known.

You will be painting a picture of yourself through writing down what you are good at—a 'Pen Picture'.

Task:

From the checklist you have just completed, make a note of those things where you have a lot of Can Do's.

Then make a list of those things, which you need help with. The third list is those things, which you find difficult.

Use the space below or your notepad or word processor.

Can Do.

Can do with help.

I find these difficult.

You will now be able to see what positive qualities you can match up to job descriptions. It is no use applying for a job for which you are clearly unsuitable—at this time. However, there is no reason why you can't hang on to your dreams and find ways of improving where you need to so that, one day, you can release your potential and realise your dreams.

You will need to carry out this last task for both the Personal Skills Checklist and the Work Skills Checklist.

One more thing before we finish. Ask someone who knows you, what qualities they think you have. Show them your list; you might be surprised at their answers. Often others can see things in us that we can't ourselves.

Goal setting.

Now that you have seen what various job requirements are and looked at your own skills and qualities, you may have to revise your current expectations of your place in the job market.

Do not lose sight of your dreams! You will get there one day but perhaps not in the way you thought you would.

Time now for some goal setting.

1.Take a sheet of paper and write at the top:

What I want to do/be one day.

2.List one or two things you have thought about.

3.Set a long-term goal for achieving this. It may be that you have to do something else on the road to achieving your goals but do not lose heart. No learning is ever wasted.

4.Set some short-term goals. Looking at jobs on offer, which fit loosely with what you would like to do, and comparing what skills you are likely to need with the results of your checklist, try and identify what you will have to do in order to improve. These will be your short-term goals.

Don't forget to put a date when you think realistically, you will do this by, and how/where, you will do this.

This is a blank sheet for you to draw your own picture so to speak.

Check your knowledge.

Write your answers in the space below without looking back on the chapter.

1. What are the benefits of taking some work experience or voluntary work? Name two.

2. Where you can find information about jobs on offer? Name as many as possible.

3. Name three personal skills from the list that you can do without help.

4. Name three work skills from the list that you can do without help.

Now you can go back and check your knowledge!

You have identified some current skills and have set goals. You are now ready to move on to applying for a job.

Signposting to QCF.

Relationship of this chapter to the knowledge and understanding of other qualifications.

SSA 14.1 Foundations for Learning and Life. 14.2 Preparation for Work.

City&Guilds Award and Certificate in Employability and Personal Development (7546)

- ➤ Effective skills, qualities, and attitudes for learning and work.
- ➤ Positive attitudes and behaviours at work.
- ➤ Searching for a job.
- ➤ Recognising employment opportunities.
- ➤ Self-Assessment.

OCR Personal Life Skills. Employability Skills.

- ➤ Assessing myself for work (Shared Unit).

OCR Employability Skills.

- ➤ Learning about a range of opportunities in work.

Functional Skills English.

- ➤ Reading.

Essential Skills Wales Communication.

- ➤ Reading.

Wider Key Skills (Wales only).

- ➤ Working with Others Part A What you need to know. Part B What you must do

.

Chapter Two. Job Applications

You have found the perfect job and want to apply for it. Great! But how do you go about that? In this chapter we will look at different ways of applying for a job, how to structure a CV. and preparing for an interview.

Many job vacancies advertised will ask you to complete an application form. Some large organisations will not accept a Curriculum Vitae or CV, as they are known.

They have their computer systems set up so that they can input the information to their own requirements; also to ensure that they can compare all the applicants fairly, with the least possible delay.

They can also find out if you can follow instructions and there is usually a space at the end to expand on aspects not covered in the application form. In addition, they like to see how well you can write and make sure that the application is in your own hand and written by you.

They are usually quite specific in how they want the information to be laid out and if you do not follow these instructions, your application will simply be thrown out—no matter how good or suitable you are, as you are demonstrating that you can't follow instructions.

Some organisations will not even accept a covering letter but this is quite unusual. A brief letter makes the application personal. So look carefully at what the advertisement says. If it says 'application with covering letter' then you must send one. In general, unless there are specific instructions not to send a covering letter, then it should be safe to do so.

Other organisations however, welcome a well-prepared CV with a covering letter. This allows you to give a more personal flavour to your application and them to find out a little more about you as the way in which you craft your CV says a lot about you.

In either case, if you have an up-to-date CV it is easier to complete accurately an application form from this, as it should have all the information you need to include—in whatever form you are asked to. So now, we will look at writing a CV and covering letter, how to structure a CV, Pen Picture & strengths/weaknesses, and going for an interview.

Writing a CV and covering letter.

Some points to remember:

Put your name, address, telephone number and e-mail address at the top of the letter. If you have reasonable ICT skills, you might like to tailor one of the letter templates on Microsoft Works, or on-line through Microsoft Word. This looks professional. Whatever you do it is important that the person reading your application can find your contact details easily.

Be brief. The bulk of the information is in your CV.

> ➤ Name and address to whom the letter is intended.

> ➤ Address the person to whom you are writing, by name. Mr./Mrs./Miss if possible. Do not be over familiar.

> ➤ Refer to the advert and where you saw it but don't say 'I am writing . . ..' We know you are! Instead, be positive about your reason for wishing to be considered and refer them to the full information in your CV (This is called a call to action.) e.g. 'In response to your advertisement in the Motown Chronicle, I wish to be considered for the post of . . .' The reason for saying where you saw the advert is that the organisation would most likely want to know which adverts get the most response.

- ➢ Look at what the job entails and state briefly how you meet those requirements.

- ➢ Show that you know a little about the company and refer briefly, as to how your skills/interests match up to this. You need to catch their attention.

- ➢ End by reminding them where you can be contacted and that you look forward to meeting them. (Be positive.)

- ➢ Again, http://www.totaljobs.com has some good advice and letter templates can be found on Microsoft® Works or Microsoft® Word on-line.

It is important however, that your own personality comes through in your reply.

Task:

Overleaf is a sample outline.Take a look.

[Your Name[

[Address and postcode]

[Phone incl. STD code]

[e-mail:]

[Date and year]

[Recipient Name]

[Street Address]

[City, County Postal Code]

Dear

Re: [here name the position for which you are applying]

I read with interest your vacancy for a   in the and enclose my application for consideration.

[Go on to show that you know something about the organisation and briefly how you would be an asset to the firm]

I am available for interview at your convenience and look forward to hearing from you.

Yours sincerely,

[Leave a space for your signature but type your name underneath.]

If you use one of the templates mentioned above, you can simply click on the various parts and fill in the detail.

If you can't type up a letter, do not despair. A neat, handwritten one is perfectly acceptable. Black ink is better. Just follow the guidelines above.

How to structure a CV.

(Adapted from *Release Your Potential: Making Sense of Personal and Professional Development*. Marsh 2011)

In general, you will need to tailor your CV depending on your situation. e.g.:

> School leaver or completed further /higher education.

> Wanting a career change.

> Returning to work after a break.

You might find that a qualifications-based CV is more suited than a skills-based one. There are many specific jobs-based templates in Microsoft Word. In this book, I aim to show you an example which you can adapt.

Pen Picture. Strengths and Weakenesses.

Task 1:

Identify 10 positive words to describe yourself.

....

....

....

Identify 10 negative words to describe yourself.

....

....

....

Task2:

Look again at Personal and Work Skills Checklist. It would perhaps be a good idea to build the more positive ones into your pen picture or personal profile for your CV

Prospective employers see this section first so it must have impact. It must ensure that the person scanning the applications will put *your* CV in the 'must see' pile and be included in the short list.

Task 3:

Using the example in the sample CV overleaf, construct a short sharp 'pen picture' or 'profile' using your 10 positive words. The rest of the CV can be filled later but remember there is no need to put your date of birth, your marital status or how many children you may or may not have. It is your suitability for the job, which matters. Prospective employers can work out your age from your CV.

Do not put any confidential information, such as your National Insurance Number, under any circumstances as you could lay yourself open to identity theft.

If you are between jobs or looking to go for something better, you may be a member of a professional organisation, (e.g. you may be undertaking a qualification that gives you affiliated membership such as the Institute of Leadershship and Management). If so, it is well worth including this on your CV—even though affiliated status does not normally allow you to put designated letters after your name—as it demonstrates your commitment to your development and upskilling. If you have achieved a qualification, which allows you to join a professional organisation, again I would advise you to do so. The organisation will tell you if there are any designated letters, which you can put after your name. It is important to include any which are applicable as this demonstrates that you are up to date. Professional organisations normally have a periodic journal, which they send to members with articles, which keep them up-to-date with issues in their area of work.

(At the time of writing, these professional membership fees are tax deductable.)

It is important that you have all your work and education properly laid out and updated on a regular basis.

This not only allows you to have a snapshot in front of you of what you have done; it is handy to have one to hand when a suitable position comes up, especially if the deadline is close; and especially if you have to complete an application form without too much stress.

If you are just setting out on your career path—you may have just left school—your CV may be quite basic. Do not worry about this. Write about yourself and what you have done. If you have someone who can help you, then ask them. Very often, other people can see qualities in you that you either don't or would be too shy to put down on paper.

Curriculum Vitae of < Name >.

(Also, add any professional designatory letters or degree after your name.)

Personal Profile. (Example)

I am an organised, enthusiastic, and committed individual who has demonstrated accomplishments in the areas of *<here put whatever relates to you>*.

I am a motivated individual with good communication skills and a flexible attitude who works well in a team. I have contributed in a positive way to the work of my department *< give an example if possible>*. Recently I have *<here insert something positive you have done>*. My current position as a < . . . >, requires me to apply method, attention to detail and interpersonal skills.

In my spare time, I am a member of my local amateur dramatic society, which relies on teamwork.

Personal Information.

Address: E-mail:

Tel: Mobile:

Professional Memberships. (If none, leave out.)

June 2008—to date   Institute of Customer Service Member.

Education. Training. Professional Qualifications.

Date: (most recent first)   Awarding Body and subject.

If you are working towards a qualification, include this before anything you have already achieved. If you are undertaking an apprenticeship which has lots of different parts (e.g. the Technical Certificate or taught part of the course which provides the knowledge and understanding or the NVQ/Key Skills etc.) then list the name of the Apprenticeship and then all the components.

Don't forget to list your GCSE and GCE A-level results — highest grade first.

Include any achievements from school e.g. Princes Trust Award/Duke of Edinburgh Scheme/Health and Safety or First Aid Certificates.

Employment Experience. (Most recent first.)

Date: Organisation. Address.

                               Position.

This involved—(Here give a general overview of your duties.)

Achievements—(Here give any successes your department achieved or targets you reached. Include your personal contribution.)

Date: Organisation. Address.

                               Position.

This involved—(Here give a general overview of your duties.)

Achievements—(Here give any successes your department achieved or targets you reached. Include your personal contribution.)

If it is not long since you left school or worked, do not forget to include any part-time or casual work. What you include in this section depends on your circumstances.

If you are further on in your working life you may want to make the earlier positions briefer.

If you have had a number of part-time or short-term jobs, you could combine them all together by saying for instance:

1998—2003 I worked in a variety of jobs in . . .

This would show that you are flexible and willing to work.

Personal Interests and Activities.
Here you could include any clubs or organisations of which you are a member. This helps to give your prospective employer a brief insight into you as a person and what other qualities you demonstrate that you could bring to the job role.

References are available on request.
Do not include references unless the job description asks for them. These will be asked for if the employer wants them.

If the job adverts says that you must provide names of referees, include them here but make sure that you ask their permission first.

Signature: Date:
Include a footer in the document with the date so that you know when it was updated.
You now have the basis of your own Curriculum Vitae (CV).

Overleaf is a sample of what it could look like.

Curriculum Vitae of A. N. Other.

Personal Profile.

> [blank box]

Personal Information.

Address.	E-mail.
Tel:	Mobile.

Professional Memberships.

Education. Training. Professional Qualifications.

Date.	Awarding Body and Subject and Grade.

Employment Experience.

Date From—To   **Organisation. Address.**
                                      Position.

This involved—

Achievements.

Date From—To   **Organisation. Address.**
                                      Position.

This involved—

Achievements.

Personal Interests and Activities.

References are available on request. (Possibly give two names.

Signature: Date:

Of course, you are free to construct yours in any way that you wish. The guidelines above are, however, tried and tested.

Task 4:

Go to http://www.totaljobs.com/careers-advice/cvs-and-applications/personal-statement and look at the examples.

Check your CV here to see if you have covered everything:

http://www.totaljobs.com/Contents/cvchecker.aspx

Take a break now and think about what you have learned so far in this chapter.

Read over your CV, sleep on it, and go back to it. Do you need to change anything? If something comes to you when you least expect it—make a note.

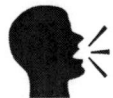

Show it to someone you can trust e.g. a family member or teacher. In this world of hundreds of applications for one job, keep your intentions about applying for a job as confidential as possible so that someone who has overheard you discussing it will not jump in, apply for it, and beat you to the winning post! It sounds hard but it really is a jungle out there.

Going for an Interview.

One morning, the eagerly awaited letter arrives on the doormat. You have been selected for an interview! Well Done!

Full of excitement and anticipation you make a note in your diary and leave it at that. Right?

Wrong!

You have a lot of preparation to do before THE DAY.

<u>Some point to consider when going for an interview.</u>

How will I get there? Bus, train, car, get a lift off someone? You need to be sure that you can travel to work without any problems so it would be a good idea to do a dummy run beforehand if you can. If travelling by bus, check the bus timetables and any connections. If you live a distance from the organisation, they will want to be sure that you can get to work on time, especially if the job involves odd hours. It certainly would not do, in any case, to arrive late for the interview. It is much better to be self-sufficient and not rely on other people for getting to work.

It is far better to have this information to hand when they ask the question.

Do I need a haircut? Do this in good time to allow your hair to settle in afterwards.

What will I wear? Even if you are going for a manual job, a suit is never out of place. If you don't have a suit and are unable to get one, a shirt and tie is an absolute must with a smart pair of trousers (male). You could then perhaps get away with a smart casual jacket. For the ladies, a suit is always suitable with a nice blouse—no low-cut tops please! It is however not just an interview for the job, but for your future. A good rule is to dress for where you want to go to, what you want to be. Dress to impress is another maxim and very true as first impressions really do count.

Do my clothes need cleaning/washing/pressing? Get this organised in good time.

Have I looked on the Internet for information on the company? I do need to impress them.

What kind of questions will I be asked? You will most certainly be asked why you want to work in the organisation, why you want the job or even what makes you think that you are suited for it. Have this information ready.

You may be asked about the organisation, for instance, what they do.Have you researched on the Internet? Do you have some notes ready? There is more on the sort of different questions that you may be asked on the following website—http://www.direct.gov.uk/en/Employment/Jobseekers/Hel papplyingforajob/DG_173785

Have I got all my Certificates and/or Record of Achievements (School), or CPD Portfolio ready?
(For CPD see *Release Your Potential: Making Sense of Personal and Professional Development.* Marsh 2011)

Do I know which part of the building I have to go to, who I have to ask for, and what their position is?

Check your letter and if needs be, ring up and ask for the department who sent out the letter and ask anything you are not sure about. If nothing else, it breaks the ice and gives you the opportunity to introduce yourself. You now become a person. Not just another name.

Task: ✎

Think of **three** examples of good practice when attending an interview.

1.

Why? What is the reason?

2.

Why? What is the reason?

3.

Why? What is the reason?

Think of **three** examples of bad practice when attending an interview.

1.

Why? What is the reason?

2.

Why? What is the reason?

3.

Why? What is the reason?

Task:

Find **three** pieces of information, which you can use to support your application for a job. It must be relevant.

1.

Why? What is the reason?

2.

Why? What is the reason?

3.

Why? What is the reason?

Did you follow the link earlier about the kind of questions you may be asked?

Take another look and pick out those that apply to the job for which you are applying. Answer them below or on a separate piece of paper. This is not a test. It is designed to prepare you for what could be the most important meeting of your life.

Question 1

Answer.

Question 2

Answer

And so on . . .

On the day of the Interview.

> ➤ Get up bright and early. Allow yourself plenty of time. Hopefully you will have been able to book a day's holiday from work or changed your shift. Do not just phone in sick. This is a common ruse and employers can usually see that you are not being honest. You do want a reference don't you?

> ➤ If the interview is in your own organisation, you will need to speak to your line manager to arrange some time off in the day.

> ➤ A good breakfast will set you up for the day. A shower and clean hair is essential. Don't forget deodorant and clean teeth! You did get an early night didn't you? Or did you go out and come home the worse for wear? If so—bad move!

> ➤ Dress carefully allowing yourself plenty of time to catch your bus or train or to get through traffic. You have planned your route haven't you? You need to arrive in plenty of time to get through any security or checking-in procedures.

> ➤ Many organisations have a security gate. If so, the security guard usually has a list of people expected. They will tell you where to go. You will probably be directed to the reception area. Here the receptionist will take your name, and usually ask you to take a

seat while someone comes to escort you to the interview room. This will be part of their security procedures.

> While you are waiting, go over your notes about the job—how will your qualities help the organisation to prosper. Take deep breaths. Remember the three C's—cool calm and collected. If there are other interviewees in the room, do not give anything away. Stay in your own space. A smile of greeting is enough.

When your turn comes:

> Head up, shoulders back and smile, smile, mile! If your head is up your rib cage lifts. You can breathe better and as your chin will be up, you will communicate better and more clearly. A smile on your face comes through in your voice.

> Answer the questions clearly and calmly. Perhaps bring out a piece of information on what you have done e.g. certificates, to clarify and expand on a point. Did you prepare some notes to help you refresh your memory beforehand? Be positive. If asked about your last job, focus on the things you did well.

> You will probably be asked if you have any questions. Did you remember to prepare some?

> How much will you be paid—the advert may have given a salary range.

> Holidays? Sick Pay? On-the job training? What opportunities are there to advance in the organisation?

These are just a few points. Again, the website www.direct.gov.uk is a good source of information with many useful links.

Check your knowledge.

Write your answers below without looking back on the chapter.

1. In which order should your jobs/qualifications be listed on your CV?

   a)Current or latest first and work backwards to school? Y/N

   b)Leaving school to the present day? Y/N

2. What is an employer looking for in an interview?

3. You should find out about the organisation that is advertising. Why?

Now you can go back and check your knowledge!

In this chapter, we looked at identifying what employers are looking for, looking at job vacancies, identifying personal skills and qualities, a self-assessment checklist, what do I need to do better/learn?

You will hopefully be more confident in applying for a job and attending an interview.

**Now might be a good time to think about how you use social media, i.e. your Facebook Page and Twitter. It is easy for an employer to find you. Do you give a good impression of yourself in the way in which you communicate with others? I came across an e-book (29 pages), which brings home how a bad social media page can cost you a job. The link to this Kindle book is at the end of this book under 'Links'. If you do not have a Kindle e-reader, download the free Amazon Kindle app. to your computer.

Signposting to QCF.

Relationship of this chapter to the knowledge and understanding of other qualifications.

SSA 14.1 Foundations for Learning and Life.

14.2 Preparation for Work.

C&G Award and Certificate in Employability and Personal Development 7546.

- ➢ Career planning and making applications.
- ➢ Applying for a job.
- ➢ Preparing for an interview.
- ➢ Interview skills.
- ➢ Getting to a destination safely and on time.
- ➢ Self-Assessment.

OCR Personal Life Skills.

- ➢ Identifying and making personal decisions.

OCR Employability Skills.

- ➢ Preparing for and learning from interviews.
- ➢ Presenting personal information effectively.

Functional Skills English.

- ➢ Reading.
- ➢ Writing.

Essential Skills Wales Communication.

- ➢ Reading.
- ➢ Writing.

Chapter Three.
Working Effectively in the Workplace

Working effectively in the workplace? Hmm! What does that mean? You may say:

'I know how to work with other people. I mean, we stand there and chat and take our time with jobs. We have a great laugh. Sometimes, I am a bit late but my pals cover for me until I sneak in.'

Right? Wrong! Of course, it is important that you enjoy your work but there is more to it than that. Working effectively in the workplace starts when your alarm bell goes off in the morning, or someone calls you that it is time to get up.

It is important that you work effectively with your colleagues and supervisors otherwise orders would not be met. Customers would be lost and, in the end, your employer would not be able to pay your wages. You would not have a job anymore. You must be able to show that you are a reliable person to employ. How do you do this?

In this chapter, you will learn about:

➢ Attitude and behaviour.

➢ Getting to work.

➢ Effective communication.

➢ Working effectively.

Please go to the next page where we will look first at acceptable levels of attitude and behaviour.

Attitude and behaviour.

In this topic, we will cover:

- ➤ Behaviour in work.
- ➤ Following codes of conduct.
- ➤ Being flexible and adaptable.
- ➤ Motivation.
- ➤ Being professional in work.
- ➤ Thinking about your own approach and attitude in work.

Why is it important to have a positive attitude? *Why* is it important to behave properly in work and not lark around? Can you think of one or two reasons?

Task:

Put your thoughts in the box below. No one is going to mark them. We just want you to start to think about it.

1.

2.

3.

What would happen if you thought you could just turn up, work at a slow speed, waste time, and generally be sloppy in work? Well, you wouldn't last very long! Your colleagues would soon get fed up of covering for you and doing your work. After all, they don't get paid extra to do your work and they have their own timescales and quotas to meet.

If you show a willingness to do whatever task you are given, ask for more work when you have done the tasks given, are friendly and helpful, then you will please your employer/supervisor and soon become a valuable member of the team. You may be given more responsible work to do, along with more pay. That means more goodies in life—nice clothes, holidays, better place to live etc. More importantly, you will have a feeling of achievement and self worth which can only be good for your confidence and self-esteem.

It is hard starting at the bottom or taking a job which you think is beneath you but we all had to start somewhere and sometimes—especially in the case of temporary jobs—it is a kind of long interview so that the firm can see if you fit in.

So be positive and look to the future. Be a 'Winner' and look up to where you are going.

Task: ✏️

Give an example of when your behaviour has been positive.

How was it appropriate?

Have you ever volunteered to do something? Y/N

When? How long ago? If not, why not?

Give an example.

Larking around in work or acting in an unsafe way would soon have you up for a talking to and possibly a verbal or written warning. Health and Safety in the workplace is everyone's responsibility and we will cover this in more detail in *Skills for Employability Part Two: Moving into Employment.*

I mention it here, as it is so important and must be emphasised at the outset. However most workplaces have what we call a Code of Conduct. That is the minimum standard of behaviour expected of you. This may be a formal written document e.g. in larger organisations, or you may just be instructed on do's and don'ts on your first day. In either case, you must follow them. The Health and Safety at Work Act (HASWA) 1974 covers employees' responsibilities and this must by law be posted up where everyone can see. Make sure you read it.

As we leave this topic, there is another aspect of attitude and behaviour, which we must talk about. Can you think what it is?

Task:

Put your answer below.

Now discuss this topic face-to-face either with one of your colleagues or fellow students, or in a group, and compare what you have learned. Make some notes.

Check Point!

What are the benefits of being a willing worker?

Why is a positive attitude important?

Yes, the above *are* important. You do want that job don't you? Even if it means starting at the very bottom? You do want to show that you are worth employing don't you?

Getting to Work.

OK, so you had a hard day yesterday and you wanted to relax. You had a shower, watched television for a little while, and then decided that you would go to the fast food outlet. You knew your friends would be there and it would be great to have a laugh and a moan and talk about the latest news.

Well, you only meant to be out for a couple of hours but, you got talking and time flew. It was later than you thought and it as late when you went to bed. You know the scenario. Maybe not you personally but you may have a friend who fits this picture. All too soon the alarm is ringing, you silence it and go back to sleep. Result? You have overslept; you have to go to the shop for milk for that all-important mug of coffee; you have missed the bus—

YOU ARE LATE FOR WORK!

Right!

Q. How do you avoid this?

A. You have to take responsibility.

This means not leaving it all to other people. You have to accept that you are in the big wide world of work and no one is going to carry you. You are an adult. So—if you have an early start, make sure you go to bed at a reasonable time and leave the late nights for the weekend or your days off. Set your alarm with enough time to have a shower, a decent breakfast—after all, you wouldn't expect your motorbike or car to run without fuel would you—and enough time to get to the bus stop or through the traffic and park.

Aim to get to work 5 minutes early. Better to be a little early that a little late, it creates a positive impression of a willingness to work. If you are delayed in getting to work then phone in and let them know. It saves your boss getting angry and impatient, especially if he has found something you didn't do correctly the previous day! Make sure you leave enough credit on your phone to make that call and, more importantly, make sure you have your work number stored on your phone. Apart from anything else, it is only common courtesy to telephone and it is what employers expect of you.

Appropriate dress and personal hygiene is important so make sure you have clean socks/stockings, underwear and shirt/blouse each day. If there is a uniform make sure it is clean. This is the first impression that others have of the organisation be it other employees or customers.

If there is not a uniform (for instance, a DIY chain may issue trousers, polo shirts and sweatshirts with the company logo) then remember that what is OK for the beach or a night out is usually *not* acceptable in the workplace. So no bare midriffs, skimpy t-shirts, too tight trousers, scuffed trainers or shoes etc.

Casual does not mean scruffy! Smart dress, clean skin and well-brushed hair is what we are about. It is a fine balancing act.

Check Point!

Why should you telephone your employer if you are going to be late for work or absent?

Why should you arrive for work a little earlier than your start time?

What types of clothes are not suitable for work?

Effective Communication.

What do we mean by 'communication'?

A search on the Internet provides the following explanation:

> *'Communication is a process whereby information is enclosed in a package and is channelled and imparted by a sender to a receiver via some medium . . .. There are auditory means, such as speech, song, and tone of voice, and there are non-verbal means, such as body language, sign language, paralanguage, touch, eye contact, through media, i.e., pictures, graphics and sound, and writing.'*

(Source: http://en.wikipedia.org/wiki/Communication)

Effective communication is one of the functional or essential skills (Wales) which cover speaking, listening, reading, and writing. Here you have to demonstrate that you have the knowledge and understanding, are able to communicate in a one-to-one and group situation, know about, and use appropriate body language.

You have to show that you can listen and respond to others; that you can listen to and act on instructions, and show that you understand. You also need to be able to read and respond to information and write clearly using correct spelling, punctuation, and grammar.

Communication must be effective otherwise the message is lost. To be effective it must be accurate and use the best way of sending the message. It is no use sending an e-mail to someone if they don't bother to pick up their e-mails on a regular basis! In the same way, it is no use telephoning someone urgently and leaving a message on their voice mail if they are away on holiday and are not picking up their messages. However, a quick telephone call or speaking to someone face to face is often the quickest and best way to sort out a problem and get a quick answer.

In this topic we will look at some different means of communication both verbal or auditory (face to face in a one-to-one or group meeting, telephone, web cam) and non-verbal or written (letters, memo's, e-mail, presentations, computer print outs).

Verbal Communication.

Body language is very powerful. Therefore, verbal communication is effective as you can see the reactions of the person you are talking to; you can observe their body language and see if they are annoyed, fed-up, paying attention; interested; understand what you are saying.

You can see their facial expressions and keep eye contact, which inspires confidence in the person you are talking to, and gives them a 'feel-good' factor that you value what they have to say and shows them that you are paying attention.

They can also see your body language. By making sure that you listen to what they have to say and show that you understand, you will be more effective.

For example, in the workplace or at home when you are given some instructions on a task you have to do show that you are listening, ask questions if you do not quite understand and clarify what has been said. Do not stand with your arms folded. You may be in your comfort zone when you do this, especially if you are not very confident and shield yourself. However, others may see this as defiance.

If you are taking a message, one way round this is to have a pen or pencil with you and something to write on and make notes. This will show a sense of responsibility and give you something to do with your hands.

When discussing something, avoid pointing as this shows aggression. Be clear in your speech. Do not talk 'in your boots'. Lift your chin up, open your mouth, and let the words come out clearly, so that you do not have to repeat yourself. If you are nervous of the person you are speaking to, take a deep breath to calm yourself. No one can hear you if you mumble or speak in the local dialect.

I remember when I was taking an exam when I was eleven years old and the headmistress came into the class and said:

'Girls! Remember the three 'C's'. Keep cool, calm, and collected'.

It was a valuable piece of advice and if called in to see my superior, not knowing what it was about and thinking 'Oh! What have I done now?' I have always tried to remember my three 'C's'.

If you are in a one-to-one meeting, try sitting side by side if you are working out a problem. It is more relaxed and friendly. (Did you notice how one of the main party leaders in a pre-election TV debate, always turned to his opponent when they were speaking. It showed respect and that he was listening.)

Using the telephone—some hints and tips.

Most companies have a certain procedure or 'spiel' when answering the call. At the very least, you should give a pleasant 'Good Morning/Afternoon' and say the name of the company.

If you are having a bad day, take a deep breath, put on your 'company hat', and answer in a business like way. The person on the other end forms his impression of the company from the way you speak and listen to his/her enquiry and pass on the call or take a message.

Be professional and speak clearly, as I have outlined above. Have a pen and pad ready to take down a message or make a note before you pass the call on.

Some Do's and Don'ts.

➢ Don't use slang. 'Could you hold on please', sounds better than 'hang on a sec'.

➢ Do ask who is speaking and make a note if you can't remember it.

➢ Do use their name once you have it.

- Do be positive and let them know you will find someone who can help if you can't. Don't forget to let someone know who has called.

- Don't give out information—especially personal information—unless you are absolutely sure you are supposed to. If you are not sure, as the person at the other end to hold on and go to find someone in authority. Just because someone rings up asking for information, does not mean they have a right to it. It could be a competitor!

- Do take information down correctly and check it back with the caller. If the person they want is not available, let them know you will pass on a message and get them to call back. It is useful to make a note of the time called and who they asked for.

- Do not be impatient and short with the caller. You may be in a rush to meet a deadline or be in the middle of a tricky job but the caller does not know that. If you can't handle the call—pass it on.

- Do thank the caller and say good-bye pleasantly using their name.

Remember, the caller will form an impression of you as an employee and your organisation from the way you deal with the call. After all, it could be the company chairman being a mystery caller. It has been known to happen!

Non-verbal communication.

Non-verbal communication can be held in a variety of ways.

- E-mail.
- Social networking.
- Text messages.
- Letters.
- Memos.

> Reports.

We will look in general at the most common ones you will come across whilst in work.

E-mail.

N.B. The first and most important thing to remember is that you must not use slang or the type of abbreviations you may use in a text message to your friends.

Even if your employer is only a 'one man band', the person on the receiving end does not know or even care about that. They only want an answer to their query or problem. Therefore, be professional at all times in your e-mail. Start with a salutation e.g. 'Good Morning Ian' or, 'Dear Mr. . . . .'

Only when you are on more familiar terms could you possibly start with 'Hi'. Keep to the point and be clear. Do remember to do a spell and grammar check. Read it through and sign off with 'Regards . . .' If the person is someone you are more familiar with or if the company is very laid back, you could end with 'Cheers' but be careful of using that term.

A disadvantage of using e-mail is that we tend to dash off something very quickly and if we are annoyed about something, tend to write as we feel. Remember that something you write may be taken the wrong way. The person on the receiving end cannot hear the inflection in your voice or read your body language and can easily take offence. (That is why it is sometimes better to pick up the phone!)

I have often been annoyed when someone at a level below or the same level issues an instruction such as: 'Please send this to me as soon as possible'. Much better to say: 'I would be grateful if you could send . . . to me as soon as possible.' or, 'Would you send this to me as soon as possible please?'

The last two are much more a request than an order. Your e-mail system has the facility for making folders to put e-mails in as you send and receive them. Make use of this. It is invaluable. There is more on e-mail use in Chapter Four of this book.

Social Networking and Text messages.

There are many social networking sites such as Twitter, Facebook, Linked in, and Scribd. etc. You only have to visit a website and click on the 'share' button to see there is a whole raft of them. Your organisation may have a Facebook business page or a Twitter account.

If you are in a position to use these on behalf of your organisation, it is imperative that you do not abuse the Terms and Conditions. So, no abusive language, no personal digs at people, no slang, etc. etc. On Facebook, you do not have a limit to words, so it is easy to get the message across. With Twitter, you are limited to 140 characters and this is not so easy.

As in all communication, use the **KISS** principle.

Keep **I**t **S**hort and **S**imple.

The Facebook 'business page' may be linked to Twitter in which case the message goes from Facebook to Twitter. Any extra length in the message is converted into a link which, when clicked, takes the reader to the original message. Again, remember that the person reading your posts may not know your sense of humour and something you think is a joke could be taken the wrong way and seem offensive.

Many people use a kind of shorthand on Twitter but really, this is just not on. Apart from destroying our beautiful English language, it is sloppy to say the least. Use proper grammar and punctuation. How you write says a lot about you and you do want to get on don't you?

One other point to remember. Messages on social networking sites can quickly spread to people for whom they may not be intended, by use of 'share' and 're-tweet'. Think what impact this could have, not only on your organisation but yourself, whether you are using them in work or personally.

Letters, memos, and reports.

Most organisations have letter headed paper and unless you are working in an office, you probably would not have to send out letters. This goes for a report that is normally dealt with by someone in a high position or a specialised role. You do however; need to know that they exist.

At some stage, you may be asked to send out a memo. This is an internal method of communication. Very often, you will find them pinned to the notice board in the staff canteen.

A memo will briefly show: who it is from; who it is to; date; subject. It will probably be only a few sentences or paragraphs. It will be signed. It will say who is to receive a copy.

See example.

Memorandum.

To: All Employees.

CC: Office Manager.

From: Joe Standing.

Date: 12th January 2012

Re: Rubbish in canteen.

The canteen is very untidy and messy. It is so bad that it has become a health and safety issue.

Please ensure that you use the rubbish bins provided.

Please wipe the microwave out if you spill something and put the milk back in the fridge.

Likewise, please wash your mugs out and put away.

The canteen is a rest area and for the benefit of everyone.

Please leave it as you would wish to find it so that we can

all enjoy our breaks.

Thank you for your co-operation.

J.A.M. Sand.

Works Manager.

As in all written communication be it a formal letter/memo, Twitter, Facebook or sending text messages, make sure that you use proper spelling, grammar and punctuation. You may be the lowest of the low now but that is the first rung of the ladder. People take notice and judge by what they see.

Task:

Think back to a message that you had to pass on to someone or a letter you had to write. It might only have been a simple, short one. Complete the short questions and answers overleaf.

Checkpoint questions	Put your answer here.
Who are you communicating with?	
What do you have to tell them?	
Why?	
What method will you/ did you use?	
When do/did you have to complete the task?	
Where is the message/ letter to be sent?	

Does this help?

If you wish to type up your answers on the computer, that is fine—go ahead.

The topics in this section are covered in more detail in many other publications and on the Internet. This book simply aims to touch on the basics.

Check Point!

Why is it important to use proper grammar when sending e-mails etc?

What is body language?

List three types of non-verbal communication.

That was a big section. Take a short break now and gather your thoughts.

Working Effectively.

Before you start this topic, let us take a moment to stop and reflect on the learning so far. We have covered some quite basic—what may seem irrelevant—topics. Believe me; they are there for a purpose.

Many of you will say 'but I know all that'. Good. That's brilliant. However, there are many who do need the reassurance that the standards laid down here are what are needed if they are to become and remain employable. So from the starting block we are three quarters way down the track and nearly at the finishing line of this chapter.

We will now move on and discuss how to work effectively.

When you are given a task to do, there are some things to think about if you are going to carry it out in the time allowed and above all safely. First, you need to plan how you are going to carry out the task you have been give. It is no use gathering all your tools and then finding that you can't reach the job because you need a ladder. You then have to go back and collect one! Does this sound familiar? As in all things, carrying out a task falls into three parts:

➢ Planning what you have to do

➢ Carrying out the task

➢ Looking back over the task to see what you could have done better

Working together with other people involves taking into consideration what they are able to do; giving them some respect; being pleasant, willing and flexible; listening to the instructions and making sure that you all know and understand which part of the task each of you have to do. This will be covered in more detail in *Skills for Employability Part Two: Moving into Employment (The Business Environment)*.

For now, we will look at a task you are going to do on your own.

Planning what you have to do.

You will be given some instructions. Make sure that you understand exactly what you have to do. Make notes if possible and ASK if you are not quite sure of anything. I know, it is awful if you are new and shy and don't want to appear foolish. You will look more foolish if you do it all wrong and possibly cost your boss a lot of money.

Think about the materials, equipment, and/or tools you will need. This includes any personal protective equipment such as gloves, a hard hat, overall, and other equipment such as a trolley or stepladder etc. Do you need any hazard warning signs? You are required by the Health and Safety at Work Act to:

> ➤ Take reasonable care for your own health and safety and that of others who may be affected by what you do or do not do.

> ➤ Co-operate with your employer on health and safety.

> ➤ Correctly use work items provided by your employer, including personal protective equipment, in accordance with training or instructions.

> ➤ Not interfere with or misuse anything provided for your health and safety or welfare.

(Source:http://www.worksmart.org.uk/rights/my_employer_has_given_me_prot ective_clothing)

Health and Safety is covered in more detail in *Skills for Employability Part Two: Moving into Employment (Introduction to Health and Safety in the Workplace)* but for now you might want to take a look at http://www.hse.gov.uk/pubns/ppeindex.htm

You also need to be quite clear when the task has to be completed. Will you need any help? Where will this help come from? Who will you ask if something is too heavy for you to lift/move on your own? There is quite a lot to think about isn't there?

Task:

Think about the things you had to do last week. This may be from work or home

1. What did you intend to do?

2. What did you do right 'first time?'

3. What did you have to do again? Why was this?

4. What did you not have time to do?

5. Did anything waste your time? E.g. answering too many mobile phone calls or surfing the web when you should have been doing things that are more important.

Does all of the above sound familiar? Yes? Well—there is room for improvement isn't there? In work, there may be restrictions on taking personal calls and using the Internet. Make sure that you adhere to them.

Carrying out the task.

When you were given your task(s)—told what you had to do—you should have made some notes. Look at these and work out what you have to do first, second and so on. In other words, prioritise. So, make another list—a 'to do list'—putting down each part of the task in order of importance, and make a note of any tools or equipment you will need. Tick them off as you complete each part. If you are stuck and have to ask for help, make a note of who you need to ask and, if it is an explanation or further instruction, make a note of what you were told to do about the problem.

Make sure that you follow any extra health and safety guidelines that may be in place for where you are working. For instance, if you are on a construction site, there will be areas where you are not allowed to be. For example in the path of a Fork Lift Truck (FLT) or if a wagon is backing up and making a delivery. In a works, there are very often marked off walkways. Make sure you keep to these. They are there for a purpose. In an office, if you have to move a lot of old files etc. you will need a trolley. In days gone by, we would have struggled to carry these manually. This is no longer allowed as it can lead to injury.

Keep an eye on the time. Work quickly and safely without stopping to chat to your mates. If you show willingness, your boss will be pleased and give you more responsible tasks. In this way, you eventually move up the ladder and better yourself.

<u>Reviewing the task. Looking back over the task to see what you could have done better.</u>
You have now done what you think you were asked to do. Stand back and survey your handiwork. Now, **STOP**, and **THINK!**

➤ Have you put all the tools and Personal Protective Equipment (PPE) away?

➤ Have you cleaned up and brushed up away any debris?

➤ Have you left a clean and tidy area?

➤ Check your job list. Have you done everything?

➤ Have you cleaned yourself up?

Now go to the person who gave you the task—probably your supervisor—and ask them to look at what you have done. Discuss any problems you had and think about what you did and how you did it.

Could you have done things a better way? Make a note for next time.

Did you ask for help when you needed or did you struggle on?

Have you done everything according to your organisations' guidelines?

The best way in which I can demonstrate this is by using a basic outline plan—one, which I have used successfully over many years with learners from all walks of life.

Task:

On the following pages, you will find a series of simple outline documents for you to complete.

The first plan is a list of all you have to do in the working day. It may be a collection of simple tasks or it may be one big task split up into smaller parts.

The next document is to be used as a working document as you carry out the task or one of the tasks.

The final document is for you to reflect on what you have done and if you could have done things better. There is also space for comments you had from whoever gave you the task.

You may photocopy these pages. For instance, you may need one copy for all the tasks and then use one for a breakdown of each depending on the task given.

Or you may want to use a separate sheet of paper or the computer.

Jobs list (Planning)—Your organisation may already have something in place. Use that.	
Date:	Time:
Name:	(Person carrying out the task)
When to be completed by:	Is this realistic? What about breaks?

Task(s) given by:		
To Do List	To complete by	Completed & Time
Task 1		
Task 2		
Task 3		
Task 4		

Health and Safety:

Tools and equipment needed:

PPE needed:

Who to contact if I need help:

Carrying out the task.	Any problems and what I did about it.
Task 1	
Task 2	
Task 3	
Task 4	
Health and Safety Tools and equipment: PPE:	**Returned?** Yes/No Yes/No
Who I contacted for help (if any needed)and why.	

Thinking back on the task (review).	What could I have done better if anything?
Task 1	
Task 2	
Task 3	
Task 4	
Comments from the person setting the tasks.	
Tasks completed satisfactorily. Signed:	Signed:

Check Point!

Why is it important to plan what you have to do?

Name two kinds of Personal Protective Equipment (PPE).

Why is it important to look at how well you did the job or task?

If you have completed all the tasks set out in this chapter properly, we can see if you have understood the lessons in the topics.

You have learned about attitude and behaviour required in the workplace; things to think about in getting to work on time; how to communicate effectively and a little about working effectively.

In Chapters One to Three we have looked at preparing for work (looking for a job and where you fit in); how to go about getting the job you want; and working effectively in the workplace. You have come a long way in a short time haven't you?

For now . . .

Complete the Check Your Knowledge overleaf. Then it will be time to take a break before moving on to the next chapter where we will take a brief look at ICT in the workplace—e-mail, the Internet, the basics of Excel Worksheets, health and safety when using computers—and where you go from here.

Check your knowledge.

Put the answer below without looking back on the chapter.

1. What action should you take if you are delayed in getting to work?

2. Why is personal hygiene important?

3. Name three methods of communication.

4. Is it acceptable to use slang or 'text speak' in e-mails? Y/N

5. You have been given a task and don't understand one of the instructions. What do you do?

Now you can go back and check your knowledge!

Signposting to QCF.

Relationship of this chapter to the knowledge and understanding of other qualifications.

SSA 14.1 Foundations for Learning and Life.

14.2 Preparation for Work.

C&G Award and Certificate in Employability and Personal Development 7546.

> Effective skills, qualities, and attitudes for learning and work.

> Introduction to health and safety awareness in the workplace.

> Understanding business communication.

> Self-Assessment.

OCR Employability Skills.

> Preparing information effectively.

> Carrying out and learning from practical tasks.

> Learning about workplace values and practices.

Functional Skills. English.

> Speaking, listening, and communication. Reading.

Essential Skills Wales. Communication.

> Speaking and listening. Reading.

Wider Key Skills Working with Others (Wales only).

Part A What you need to know Level 1&2. Part B What you must do: WO1.1, WO1.2, WO1.3; WO2.1, WO2.2, WO2.3.

If you are working to Level 2 in Functional Skills /Essential Skills Wales then this chapter as a whole could be used as evidence in English/Communication—reading an extended document and writing.

Chapter Four. ICT Skills in the Workplace

Congratulations! You have been successful and been asked to go for that long awaited interview. It may be a for a manual job where you are not working in an office, so you think to yourself that you do not need computer skills.

Wrong! Many organisations have computers around the building. So you do need some knowledge of the basics of using a computer. You want to show your prospective employer that, even if you do not have a vast knowledge—and you don't need it for this job—you are willing to learn and build on what knowledge you have. You may be going for a job in the office of an engineering or distribution firm. Even delivery drivers and shelf pickers use computers; retail staff use computer terminals.

Therefore, in this chapter, just so that you are prepared and have another string to your bow so to speak, we are going to cover the following:

- ➢ ICT Self assessment checklist.
- ➢ E-mail.
- ➢ Internet.
- ➢ Basics of Excel spreadsheets.
- ➢ Health, Safety and Security relating to ICT.

ICT Self assessment checklist.

Before we look at some of the minimum skills you will be expected to have in most jobs, let us take a look at what you know now.

Task:

Complete the simple checklist. Some things may seem obvious but it is surprising how many people only know about the Internet or use a computer to play games.

Task	Yes	No
I know how to switch on a computer.		
I have good keyboard skills i.e. I can find all the letters, use the shift key etc.		
I am confident when using a computer.		
I can send and receive e-mails.		
I know how to search on the Internet.		
I can download documents from the Internet.		
I know how to organise files and folders in Outlook Express.		
I can set up and use a simple Excel spreadsheet.		
I can use word processing software e.g. Word/Works.		
I know how to insert images in a document.		
I know the difference between hardware and software.		
I know about health and safety when using a computer.		

If you find some of the following a little basic, I make no apologies. This book is written for all ages and abilities and I cannot assume that everyone knows everything that an employer would expect in the use of computers and Information Computer Technology (ICT). If you know most of what is in the following pages, then you will move forward faster, in the knowledge that you are up to speed.

What is a computer?

Or rather, what makes up a computer? I will attempt to give a simple non-technical explanation.

A computer is made up of various parts. Most desktop computers have a box where all the workings and connections are kept. Some are like a tower which sits easily on the top of the desk—the most convenient—or underneath, which is not so convenient as you have to bend down to get to all the connection points for other parts which connect to it.

Inside this box, there are lots of parts called components. The main one is the Central Processing Unit or CPU. This processor is the 'brain' of the computer. However, unlike the human brain which can think for itself, a computer cannot think for itself. It can only work with the information that has been input into the system, i.e. it can only *process* information that has been input into the system. The higher the specification and speed of the system, the faster information is stored and processed.

As your needs and usage increases, you don't have to buy a completely new system as you can increase the size and power of the components, although sometimes it is best to start again from scratch.

The hard drive holds all the information which has been saved by the user during operation and which has been loaded into the system from various programmes.

The memory cards determine how much and how fast it can store information while you are working. This is called Random Access Memory or RAM. If you are working with images and videos (which take up a huge amount of RAM), you need a much higher specification than you would if you just do simple documents.

Most computer systems nowadays have other drives, which can be accessed externally.

The DVD/CD drives hold discs on which you can back up information that you may want to make portable. You can also play purchased DVD/CD's. These are usually accessed via the front of the computer.

Floppy discs are not so popular now as they only hold a small amount of information. Some older computers will still have a floppy disc drive. My tower has a floppy disk drive. This is all there was until recordable DVD's/CD's and memory sticks came along. Floppy discs are a small square of hard plastic with a floppy disc inside. They only hold a very small amount of data.

More common now are portable memory sticks or flash drives that come in a variety of storage sizes. They are connected via a USB port—a very small oblong slot— either at the front or back of the computer or both. (My 'tower' only has USB ports at the back so I have a USB extension, which has four connections. This sits on the desk for convenience as I use this for backing up files to various memory sticks for different projects.)

The on-off switch is located at the front of the 'box'.

At the back of the computer are lots of slots for different kinds of connections such as the keyboard, printer, mouse, speakers, modem etc.

However, that is the basis of the computer. A laptop will have all these built in to the unit along with the display screen, a keyboard and mouse pad.

Display Screen? Keyboard? Mouse?

Yes, the computer system needs a monitor which connects to the system. Speakers, so that you can hear music and people talking, may be built in to the monitor. If not you will have separate speakers with another connection. The monitor screen, when you first switch on, is called a desktop. Quite simple really. Just as you have a physical desk, so with a computer you have an electronic desk where you put all your bits and pieces that you need to hand. (The rest are filed away, but more later.)

In order to move around the desktop or whatever programme you are using you need what is called a mouse. I suspect that this device is called a mouse as a pointer scurries around the screen as you move it. Depending on what you are doing, this pointer may be in the shape of an arrow, a straight line or a hand and changes as you work. This pointer allows you to select exactly what you want to. Just press and click on the left hand button on the mouse. A right click brings up a menu on the screen with shortcuts to other functions. Again, this small device is connected to the computer by a long thin wire. Easier to use however, is the new wireless mouse. There are fewer wires to get tangled.

Then we come to the keyboard. Again, this is connected to the back of the computer. What another connection? What if I get them all in the wrong place? Don't worry. You can't. There is a place for everything. There are also wireless keyboards.

The latest keyboards have a lot of handy buttons on them for easy access to the Internet, e-mail, sound level adjustments etc.

The main part of the keyboard is laid out like a typewriter keyboard. It is called a QWERTY keyboard. Look at the top row! Although the letters are laid out in capitals, when you type they come out as a small, or lower case, ones. To make a capital you have to press the 'shift' key. There is one on the left and one on the right of the bottom row of letters. They have an upwards facing arrow on the key. Although there are numbers along the row above the letters, there is also a set of numbers at the side, laid out like a calculator, which are easy to use. The very top row has buttons for different functions depending on what you are doing. Don't worry about that for now.

To connect to the Internet and use the e-mail system, you need a modem which you get from your Internet provider.

This is connected to the computer—usually at the back. It has lots of flashing lights.

Another important piece of equipment is the printer which, again, is connected to the computer. Nowadays, printers have a USB connection but some older ones may still have a connection called a parallel port, which is a wide blue connection with lots of pins at the end, and screws in to a different connection at the back of the computer.

On my desk, I have my tower-like box, which houses the system. (I have upgraded this as my work has become more complicated but have kept the outside shell as it has a DVD and a CD drive as well as a floppy disc drive. The DVD drive was a later addition and having two drives means that I can copy one CD disc onto a blank one. It has become part of the office.)

I have two different external microphones. One for normal recording with a USB connection and one that is connected with a 'jack', which I need to use when dubbing voice and music over camcorder film. As I said earlier, I also have an external hub of USB connections which I find useful for memory sticks, camera connections etc.

It is amazing that most of the above are crammed into a laptop and, even an even smaller net book, which has quite a small screen. All these different parts, which you can touch and feel, are called 'hardware'. Software means the different programmes, which are uploaded on to the computer.

I said earlier that a computer cannot think for itself. It can only do what it is told. With software, someone has written the programme, so it can only carry out instructions that have been written. Technology is wonderful.

I have tried to keep this explanation non-technical and non-threatening. More excellent information can be found at

http://windows.microsoft.com/en-US/windows-vista/Parts-of-a-computer

E-mail.

Most home computers use Microsoft® Outlook Express. You may work in an organisation that uses Microsoft® Outlook. This has a lot more functions than Outlook Express and is best for business use.

Just like 'snail mail 'or physical post you have a post box called an 'Inbox'. You also have an 'Outbox', which is similar to when you go to post a letter in the post box for the postman to collect and take to the sorting office for delivery.

The 'Sentbox' is where all the messages, which have left the 'Outbox' and have winged their way through cyberspace to the recipient, are stored.

There are also other folders such as deleted items and addresses, but the above are the main ones. The screen shot [Fig 1] shown is the front page of Outlook Express.

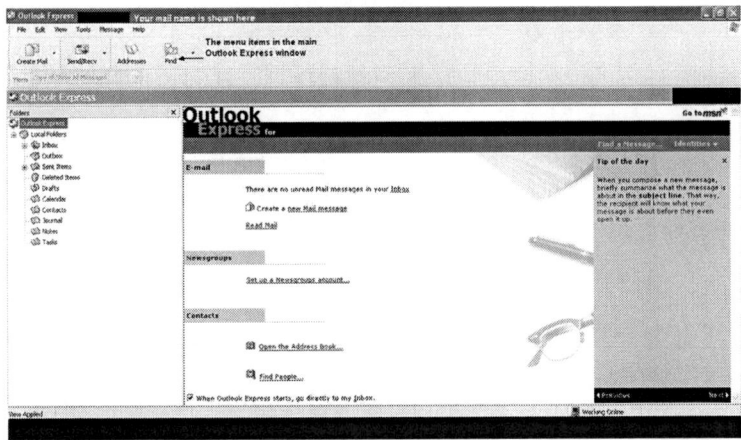

[Fig.1]

Open up Outlook Express so that you can follow what I am saying. (You may have another e-mail system but Outlook Express or Outlook are the main ones.)

The screen shot below shows you what you see on your screen when you click on the Inbox label on the left hand side of the screen. I have blanked out personal details.

You will see in Fig.2 that the list of menus has changed.

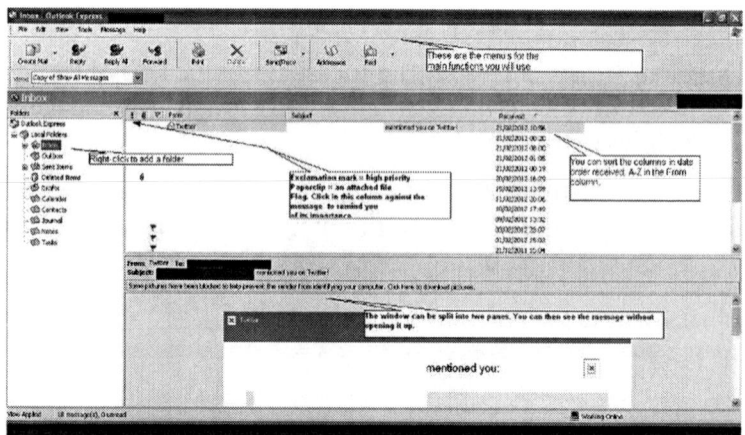

[Fig.2]

Organising your messages.

It is important to organise your e-mails into different compartments or folders. Depending on what you do, there may be a need in the Inbox for folders for the main members of the department, suppliers, subjects such as staff training etc. You would also want a similar folder in the Sentbox.

See Fig 3

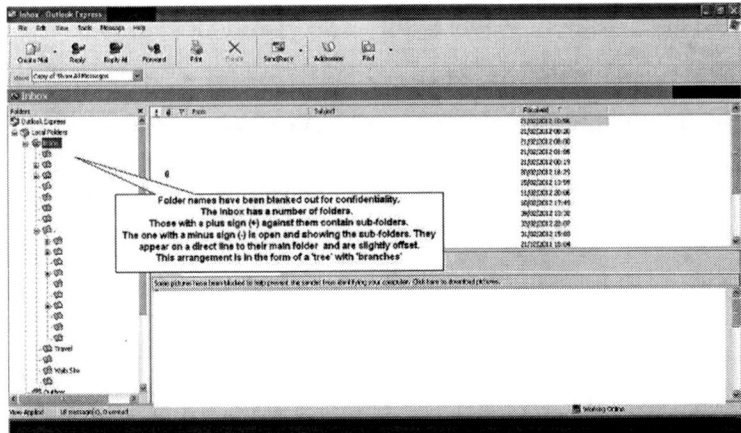

[Fig.3]

To do this:

Open up Outlook Express if you haven't already done so.

Hover the mouse pointer over 'Inbox' and right click. A small menu will show on your screen. Move the pointer down to 'New Folder' and click. A box will pop up with a space to give the folder a name. The box also shows a list of folders so that you can choose which folder in which you want to put the new one.

When you have a few folders, you may want to put some as a sub-folder to another. This box lets you do that by clicking on the folder where you want to put this new sub-folder. You can always drag and drop later from the menu at the side of Outlook Express.

You will notice that the folders within the main Inbox have a line down to them. Some of these folders in Fig.3 have a plus sign (+) next to them. This shows that there are other folders within that one. One of the folders has a minus sign (-) against it. This is because it is open and shows all the sub-folders. They are linked to the main folder by a line but you will see that they are offset.

This arrangement is like a 'tree' with 'branches'.

Do the same with the 'Sentbox'.

This is much more efficient and, when you are asked to find something, you won't have to trawl through a massive amount of e-mails. These are just the basics but there is more information at:

http://windows.microsoft.com/en-US/windows-vista/Getting-started-with-e-mail#section_5

Composing messages.

There are a number of menus in the various sections of Outlook Express for you to explore but here we will deal with the main ones.

Click on to the Inbox. Are you there? What can you see?

Does it look like the picture in Fig.4 below?

[Fig.4]

Let's take the first line.

This is quite important as using the drop down menu allows you to get the full benefit out of Outlook Express. We will take them one-by-one.

> **File.** You have choices: to start a new message, open one that is already highlighted, save a message into another folder on your computer etc.

> **Edit.** This lets you do things such as copy a message, move to another folder etc.

> **View.** This is exactly what is says. You can choose what you are able to see on the screen. See Fig 5 below. It is here that you can choose to have a preview pane. This lets you see the message without opening it in another window.

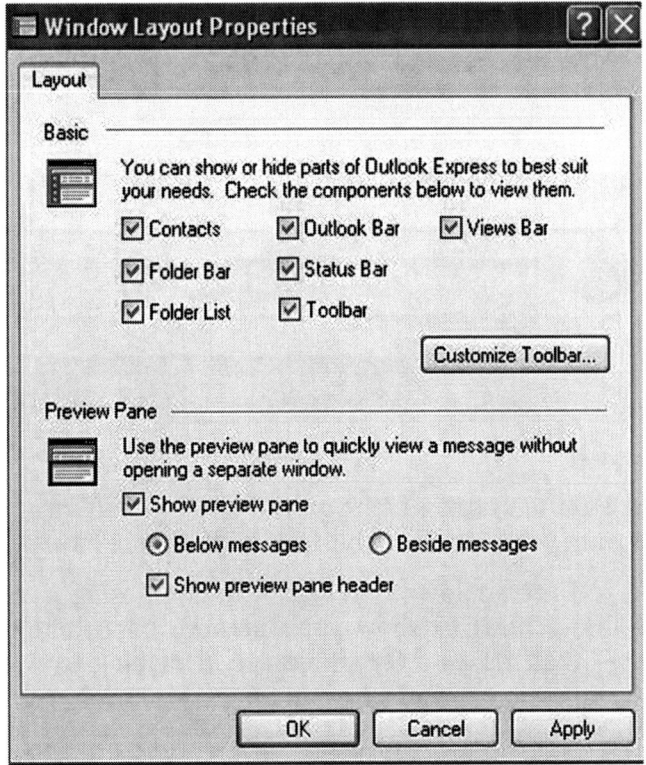

[Fig.5]

> **Tools.** This is one of the most important menus. See why below in Fig.6. Why do you think that is?

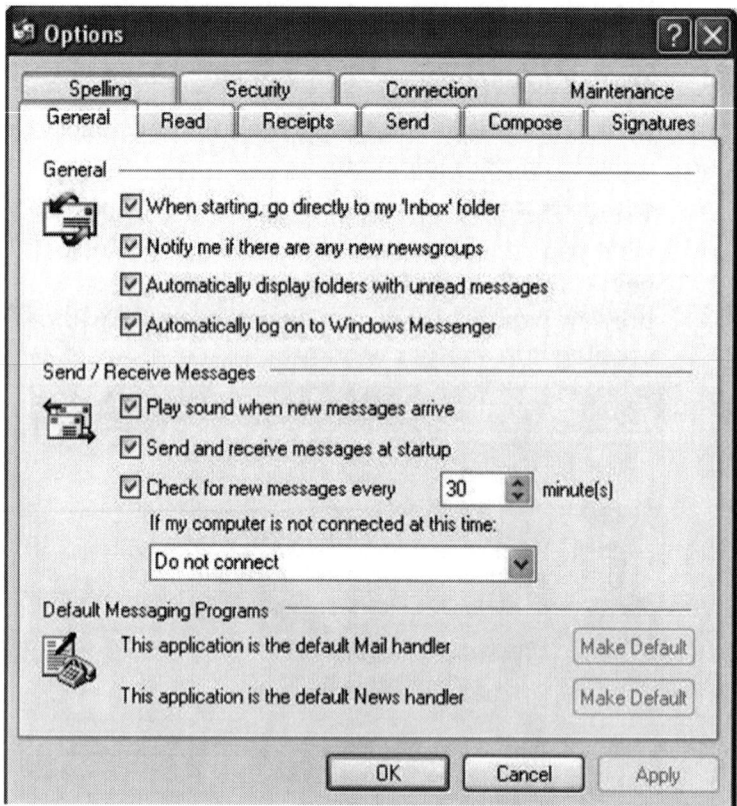

[Fig.6]

There are ten tabs, which you can click on and arrange how you want your e-mails to be dealt with. Go on, have a go!

Yes, you are anxious to get on with composing a message, but first I need to show you one very important tool—in Fig.7— that makes a big difference in making your e-mails look professional. And saves time!

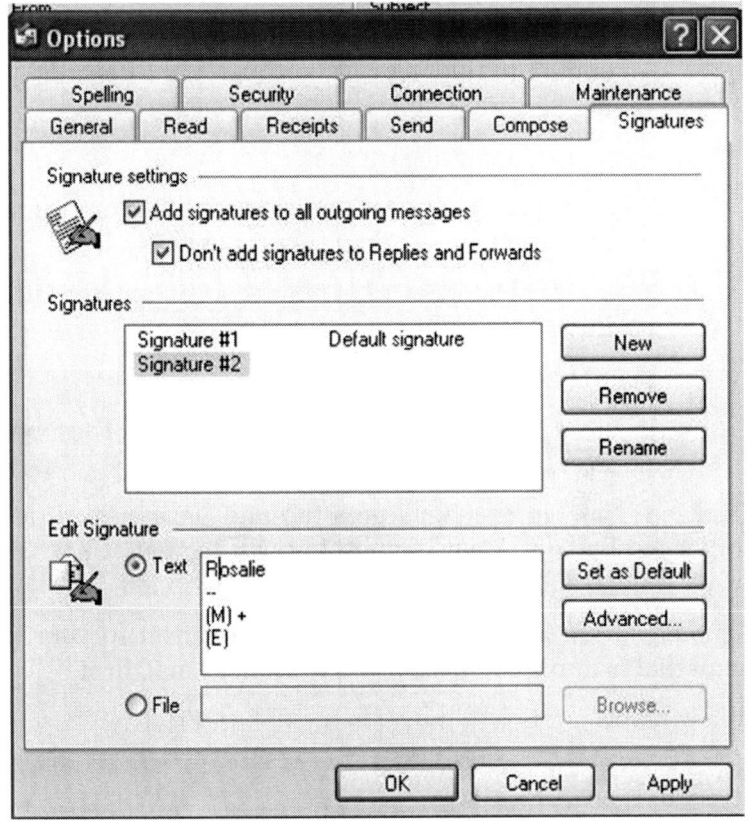

[Fig.7]

You may have noticed that some people send e-mails with what is known as a signature. In this screen shot in the Tools/Options menu, I have clicked on 'Signatures'.

This is not a written signature. At least not in Outlook Express. In a professional e-mail system such as web-based e-mail, you can add a copy of your actual signature. However, for now, we will keep it simple on a need to know basis. I have a signature for personal use with my family e-mail. This is my default signature or the one that comes up automatically with the default e-mail address. If I use another e-mail address, then I use another signature. (Signature 2 in the screen shot.)

The basics you will need are:

1. An ending to the message, such as 'Kind Regards' or 'Yours Sincerely', followed by your name.

2. Your position or department.

3. Your telephone number and extension if there is one and Fax number—again if there is one.

4. Your e-mail address. This may be a general one such as 'info @ xxx'

5. Your company web address.

6. If there is a company Twitter name or Facebook address, add these.

Click on 'New' in the signatures tab and have a go. Don't forget to click on 'Apply' or nothing will happen. Click OK when you have finished and close this menu option.

This signature adds a touch of professionalism to your e-mail that is important even if you work in a small firm.

We will now go back to the main menu bar. Fig.4

[Fig.4]

➤ **Message.** In this menu, you can decide how you want an e-mail handled. Take a look.

➤ You will see 'Block Sender' on the drop-down menu. If you get a spam or nuisance e-mail, you can block any further messages. Click on the message. Go to Messages in the menu bar and click on 'Block Sender'. (A list of blocked senders is under Tools/Message Rules/Blocked Senders List.)

➤ **Help.** This is one item, in all the menu bars of all the different software applications that people forget about.

It is, however, exactly what it says—a help menu. Ask a question and you will find a detailed answer. Take a look at Fig.8 below.

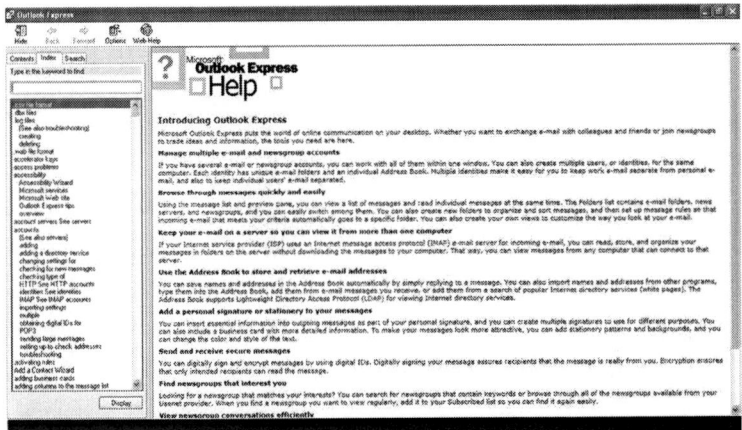

[Fig.8]

Now we will go back to the menus at the top of the screen.

Although you could go into the File menu to start a message, you can see that there is a handy icon on the second line— Create Mail. I also have other icons, which I find handy: Reply, Reply All, Forward, Delete, Print, Address Book etc.

Click on the Address Book icon and a box will pop up with a list of all your contacts. If when you add an address, you put their actual name, they will be listed under this with their e-mail address alongside. This saves you having to remember a lot of addresses when you create a message. Just type in the name.

When you are reading a message, some of these options will also come up.

Now you have become familiar with Outlook Express itself and the basics of messaging, we can move on to actually creating and sending a message. You are organised and raring to go!

On the Menu Bar, click on 'Create Mail'.

This is what you should see:

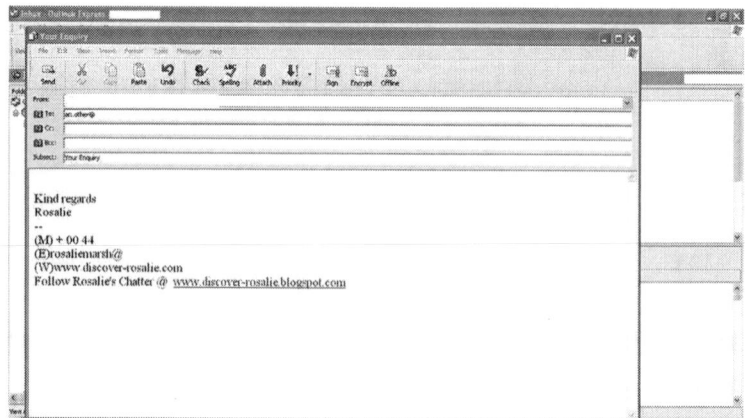

[Fig.9]

There are five lines.

The **top line** will have your own e-mail address by default.

The **'To' line** is where you type in the e-mail address for the person who will receive the message. This is called the recipient. If you have more than one person to send the message to, separate the addresses with a semi-colon (;).

As I said above, if you have put the contacts details in your address book or added them when they send you an e-mail, all you have to do is start typing the name. Much easier!

The **'Cc' line.** If you need to send a copy to someone else, for information but not exactly for them to send a reply, put their address into the 'cc.' line. This is a carbon copy.

The **'Bcc' line.** This is useful if you are sending a message to a lot of different people who are not connected and you don't want others to see their addresses, or more importantly, they wouldn't want their address shared with people they do not know. This is a confidentiality thing.

The **Subject line**. In the example I have simply put 'Your Enquiry'. This then shows at the top of the message. Make the subject brief but relevant. If it is to do with an order for instance, you could put something like the following:

Re: order Number 1234567/45 or FAO (For Attention Of) and the person's name.

The body of the message.

This is important.

In Chapter Three, I explained how important it is to speak properly in e-mails.

Task: ✎

Go back to Chapter Three. Effective Communication—Non-verbal communication—e-mail, and re-read the topic.

It starts with:

> '**N.B.** *The first and most important thing to remember is that you must not use slang or the type of abbreviations you may use in a text message to your friends.*'

Are you ready to move on and complete the message?

So, you have started politely. There may actually be a house style for e-mails. If so, make sure that you follow it.

State the reason for contacting the person and what information you need or, are providing.

End with something like:

I look forward to hearing from you.

Your signature should be there at the bottom waiting. It should say something like:

Yours sincerely, or Best Regards followed by your name and contact details as advised earlier in this chapter.

Is it ready? Is there anything else you have to do? No?

Wrong! You need to check it over. Have you said what you needed to say? Are all the spellings correct? There is no substitute for manual proofreading. However, it is also wise to run the message through the built-in spell-checker.

In the menu bar at the top, you will see an icon with **'ABC spelling** and a red **'tick'**. Click on this. You could rely on the spell-checker working when you press 'Send' but doing it this way, stops the message going into cyberspace before you are ready.

When you are sure that the message is safe to go, press **'Send'.** The message will move into the **'Outbox'** while it is being delivered. Once delivered it will show in your **'Sent'** box.

All you have to do now is to put it in the special folder you have created, if this is relevant.

Internet.

Although most people can use the Internet, there are a surprisingly number of people who can't. The reasons for this are many which include:

> ➢ Limited or no access to broadband (dial-up being too slow- live in a remote area).

> ➢ Not interested.

> ➢ Frightened of the computer—lack of confidence.

When you or your organisation wanted to install the Internet, they signed up to an Internet Service Provider or ISP. There are various ones and include TalkTalk, Virgin, BT etc in the UK. They will usually provide you with your e-mail address (see above).

Once you have logged on to your computer you will need to log on to a search engine such as Internet Explorer, Mozilla Firefox, etc. The interesting thing you will notice is that when you follow a 'link' to a site it will probably go to Internet Explorer. There is nothing you can do about this.

Each search engine has its own **'Home Page'**. You can change this to any site you like such as that of your Internet Service Provider or any other you wish. For now, don't worry about that, as your organisation will have this set up already.

When you type in a web address [Fig 10] is what the screen will look like. I typed in www.discover-rosalie.com

[Fig 10]

At the top, in the blue strip, you will see the name of the web site and the page you are on—in this case, Discover-Rosalie, and the Home page called Welcome to Just Us Two. (*Actually, you will see in this example that the actual page says 'Discover-Rosalie and Just Us Two'. That is because the front page was re-named without going behind the scenes and altering the 'back-end'. This has been changed!*) You will also see the name or logo of the ISP. In this case Mozilla Firefox.

Below that, you have the menu bar as you do in Outlook Express and other software applications.

File Edit, View, History, Bookmarks, Tools, and Help.

Task:

Log onto a computer and move your mouse cursor (the little arrow) over each of the menus in the toolbar. The **Bookmarks** menu is most useful as you can save your favourite pages for easy access later, by clicking on 'Bookmark this page'. In Internet Explorer this is called 'Favourites'.

If you are not used to a computer, don't be nervous—have a play around and become familiar with the different functions. No one expects you to know everything. It is important however, that you are familiar with the screens and are happy to explore and of course, use the Help menu when you are stuck. It is all in there.

[Fig 11]

Underneath the Menu Bar, you will see some white boxes.

The first one is called a **'tab'**. It has the name of the page you are looking at. As you move around the website and click onto other pages, this will change to the new page. At the side is a little square with a plus sign **'+'**. This is another tab. Click onto this and you will have a blank screen where you can type in another address without losing the page you are already working on. This is very useful if you are looking for information.

Underneath the tab is an arrow where you can go forward or backwards to pages which you have previously viewed.

Next to this is a long white box where you type the name of the website e.g. www.discover-rosalie.com. As you move around the site, the name in this long white box changes. For instance, if you click on the **'Events'** tab, the page comes up and the address in the long white box will be http://www.discover-rosalie.com/Just_Us_Two_Rosalie_s_Event.html and the **'tab'** title changes to Rosalie Marsh Events. This is how the site has been set up.

The white box at the right hand side is useful if you don't know the web address or you are looking for information on something. It is called a search box. For instance, you may want a job in a specific area. If you type **'jobs in Bolton'** in this search box a whole list of what we call 'search results' will come up in a new page, listing jobs in Bolton—not the whole country or rest of the world as you would get if you just typed in 'jobs'.

Go on! Try it!

Now you can see what a powerful tool the Internet is. These are just the basics. With practice, you will get more adventurous. If you have just left or are leaving school, you may have had a lot of practice in searching the Internet when researching for projects and homework. However, this may depend on the courses you have taken.

Google Chrome is another powerful search engine but it works a little different from what I have described above. It doesn't have the same menu bars for a start such as File, Edit etc. It does however, have menus for searching images, maps, You Tube, News, Gmail. If you have a Google account, when you sign in there is much more available.

One word of caution when searching for images. Remember that, before you download they may be subject to copyright!

When the search results for Google Images come up, the screen shows a lot of thumbnails. If you right-click on the mouse (the button on the right side of the mouse) and **'Save**

As', you will may be saving a thumbnail or small version. If you want to use the image in a document, you will need to click on the image to open it before you right-click and **'Save As'**. Otherwise, when you insert a thumbnail into a document and try to enlarge it will become what we call **'pixelated'** as it is being made larger than intended. Always get the best you can, reduce, and make sure you re-size corner to corner to stop it getting out of shape (what we call 'losing the aspect ratio').

You know how sometimes you see photos in a brochure and people look wider than they should be or longer and narrower than they really are? That is because they haven't been re-sized properly. When you click on an image, grab the little marks at the corner, and drag them diagonally (corner-to-corner) to make them larger or smaller. That way you should avoid the problems mentioned.

Later in this chapter, I will cover health, safety, and security relating to using ICT. For now, get onto the Internet and explore!

The basics of Microsoft® Excel.

Microsoft® Excel is really very simple. It is a huge calculator with many other functions for capturing and displaying information in basic text form or in the form of charts and images.

Whereas with Microsoft® Word, a file is the document and saved as .doc (Word 97-2003), .docx (Word 2007) etc depending on the software version, in Excel a file is known as a workbook and saved as an Excel Workbook with a file name ending in .xls (Excel 97-2003) or xlsx (Excel 2007) etc. again depending on the software version.

Although there are many other document names, you need to be aware that, although documents in Microsoft® Office (Word, Excel, Access) 2007 can read documents of an earlier version, users of Microsoft® Office 97-2003 cannot read the later 2007 Office version. This is important if you are going to share the document with someone in another organisation who may have other software/versions. If in doubt save as .xls or a *pdf file. I am working in Microsoft® Office 2007 so the Excel spreadsheet will be Excel 2007.

Excel spreadsheets simplified.

When you open up **Excel,** you are opening up a **Workbook** that you will save with a unique name so that you can find it again easily.

The **Workbook** is equal to an Exercise Book or A4 pad.

Within this **Workbook,** you can have many different **Worksheets** that are different parts of the **Workbook.** These Worksheets can all be given a different name. It is like a hardback file or ring binder having dividers or sections.

Each **Worksheet** is made up of **Pages.** Unlike a Word document, they don't show up separately, but on the same Worksheet. So just imagine a very large sheet of paper divided into smaller areas.

To follow this best, open up an Excel workbook. (I am assuming that you have turned on your computer!) Depending on how your computer has been set up, you may find the Excel icon on the Start Menu when you click on 'Start' on the bottom left of the screen. You may have to find it in the 'Programmes menu'.

Click on Start/All Programmes/Microsoft Office/Microsoft Excel. It will be called 'Book 1' by default. See Fig 12 on the next page.

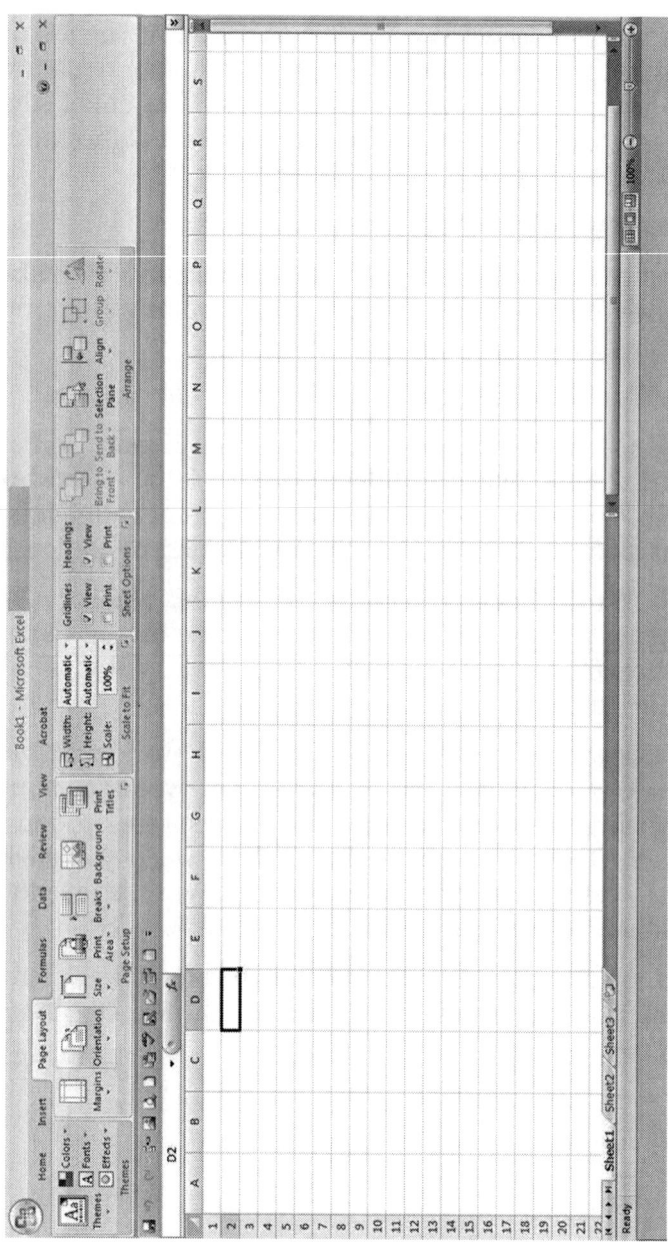

[Fig 12]

Each Worksheet is made up of little boxes called cells. One piece of information goes into each cell. The cells are named alphabetically across the top—left to right—in columns, and numerically down the left—from top to bottom in rows. Yes, this sounds a bit confusing! In the picture [Fig 12], the cursor had landed on a cell in 'column D' and 'row 2'. You will notice in the white box on the left above the cells that it says 'D2'. This cell is named D2. See left-hand box above the worksheet.

Across the top is a Menu Bar much of which is similar to Microsoft® Word. In addition, there are many tools for calculations, some of them very advanced but which need specialist training. We are concerned here with the basic use of Excel for record keeping.

I saved this workbook with the name 'Supplies 2012'. To do this, click on the coloured Office Button on the top left of the screen/Save as /Excel Workbook. *(Or File/Save As, depending on your software.)*

A window called '**My Documents**', which contains all the folders, pops up. If you want something different from the general 'My Documents folder', double left click on the folder in which you want to save the file. This will open the folder. You will see the folder icon change.

Go to the boxes at the bottom. Against **'File Name'** type in **'Supplies 2012'**. In the box below this (**'Save as Type'**), it will show **'Excel Workbook'**.

Click **'Save'**. Your work is now easily identified when you come to look for it later.

Take a look at the very simple spreadsheet overleaf of supplies for January 2012. [Fig 13]

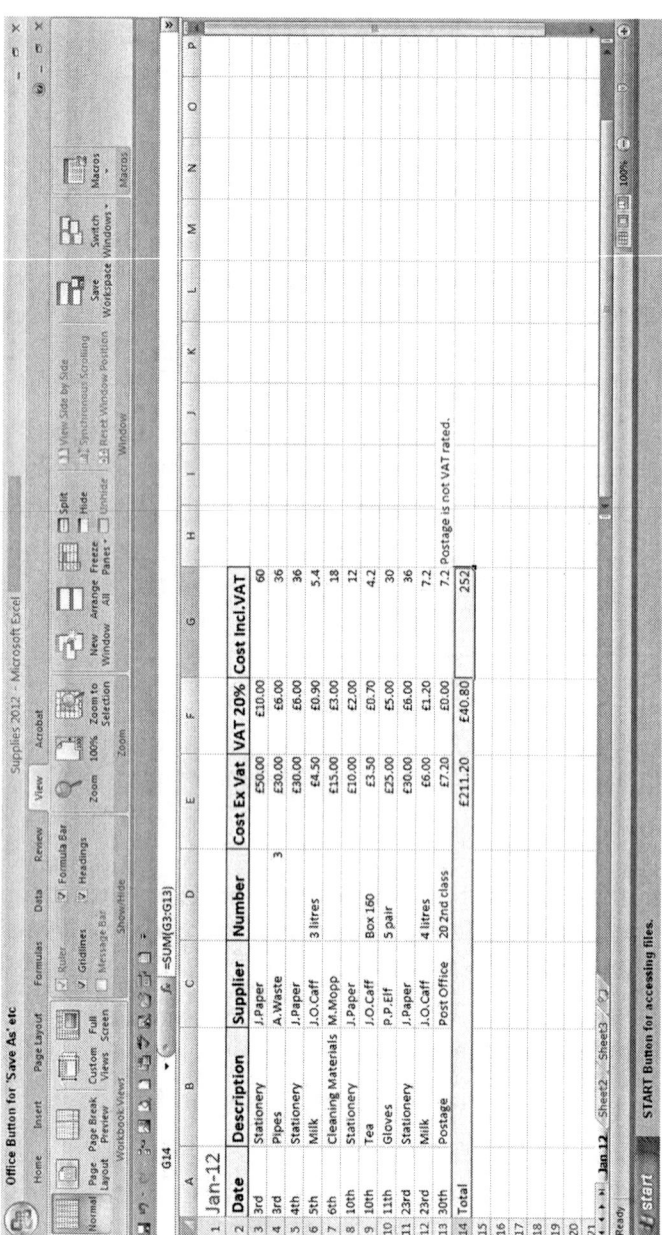

The spreadsheet shown contains:

	A	B	C	D	E	F	G
1	Jan-12						
2	Date	Description	Supplier	Number	Cost Ex Vat	VAT 20%	Cost Incl.VAT
3	3rd	Stationery	J.Paper		£50.00	£10.00	60
4	3rd	Pipes	A.Waste	3	£30.00	£6.00	36
5	4th	Stationery	J.Paper		£30.00	£6.00	36
6	5th	Milk	J.O.Caff	3 litres	£4.50	£0.90	5.4
7	6th	Cleaning Materials	M.Mopp		£15.00	£3.00	18
8	10th	Stationery	J.Paper		£10.00	£2.00	12
9	10th	Tea	J.O.Caff	Box 160	£3.50	£0.70	4.2
10	11th	Gloves	P.Elf	5 pair	£25.00	£5.00	30
11	23rd	Stationery	J.Paper		£30.00	£6.00	36
12	23rd	Milk	J.O.Caff	4 litres	£6.00	£1.20	7.2
13	30th	Postage	Post Office	20 2nd class	£7.20	£0.00	7.2 Postage is not VAT rated.
14	Total				£211.20	£40.80	252

Cell G14 = =SUM(G3:G13)

[Fig 13]

I have clicked on the 'Home' tab in the Menu Bar. This gives me most of the functions or actions, which I need at the moment.

The sheets are already named as Sheet 1, Sheet 2, and Sheet 3 with a tab, which is not named. This is where you add extra sheets if you need them.

To give each sheet a name, put the mouse cursor over the sheet tab, right click, and click on **'Rename'**. You can also change the colour of the **'tab'** (the background to the sheet name.) This is useful if you are colour co-ordinating different sorts of information. You could for instance, call the sheet— Supplies Jan.2012—and colour it red. Later we will see how you can change the appearance of the cells by formatting with tools similar to those in Microsoft Word.

I have re-named my sheet **'Supplies Jan 12'** as I wish to have a separate record or sheet for each month. I coloured it **'RED'**.

To do this, put the cursor over **'Sheet 1'** and right click on the mouse. A small menu will come up. Click on **'Rename'** and type in **'Supplies Jan 12'**. Come out of that by clicking on any cell. This saves the name and completes the action. Put your cursor back over the sheet name and right-click again. From the small menu click on **'Tab Colour'**. A small palette of colours pops up. I chose red. To complete the action, come out of this by clicking on any cell.

I decided what headings I needed on the sheet but made them **'bold'** to stand out. I used Calibri font. I gave the sheet a title of **Jan 12** in cell **A1,** for easy reference when the sheet is printed out. I made the font size larger. I coloured it **'RED'** to match the sheet name using the colour palette selection under the symbol letter **'A'** in the menu bar. (Click on the little arrow to show the colour palette.)

I decided what column headings I needed and made them **bold**: **Date, Description** (of supplies), **Number** (if applicable), **and Cost ex Vat, VAT @20%,** and **Cost including VAT.**

I wanted to make these column headings stand out and highlighted them by putting my cursor in the left hand cell and dragging it along all the columns I wanted to highlight.

Keeping the cells highlighted, I coloured the cells yellow by clicking on the arrow at the side of the paint pot and choosing yellow from the colour palette.

To make the column heading really stand out, I used the little box at the left of the paint pot to put a border around them.

I did this by keeping the cells highlighted and, clicking on the little arrow at the side of the box, chose what I wanted from the drop down selection.

This is much easier than it sounds. Try describing step-by-step how to cross a road or put a car into gear and you will see what I mean.

Under each heading, I typed in some information:

Under 'Date', I typed in '3rd'.

Under 'Description', I typed in 'Stationery'.

Under 'Supplier', I typed in 'J. Paper'.

Under 'Number', I did not put anything, as this was a mixed order.

Under 'Cost Ex VAT', I typed in 50.00.

Under 'VAT 20%', I typed in 10.00.

Under 'Cost incl. VAT', I typed in 60.00.

And so on. You can complete the spreadsheet by inputting the information as in Fig 13.

At the end of all the further entries, I Highlighted the column cells A14 -G14, coloured them yellow and put a box round as above. I typed '**Total**' in cell A14 (Date column).

The totals would go under each column of costs (E14, F14, and G14).

You will notice in Fig 13 that some of the figures have a £ sign and some don't. This is where you can format how you want the numbers to be displayed. To do this, highlight **'Column E'** by clicking on the letter **E** above all the cells. Move your cursor up to the **'Alignment'** tab on the menu bar. Can you see it? Just to the right of where you make your words Bold, centre etc.?

Click on the arrow to bring up the **Format Cells** screen. Click on **'Number'**. You can now decide if you want Currency e.g. **£** and how many decimal places, or if you just want plain numbers. I chose **'Currency'** and two **(2)** decimal places so that the **'pence'** would be displayed.

Adding up the totals.

You are probably already reaching for your calculator. You don't need it! Excel is a huge calculator with many simple and complicated functions. If you set up the following simple calculations correctly, you will save yourself a lot of work later.

So we will do a simple calculation.

Remember that I said that each cell had a name, which referred to the column letter and the row number? Well, using these you can set up a simple formula for adding the columns.

In this simple spreadsheet, we have a list of figures in columns E, F, and G. The rows go from row 3 to row 13.

The totals will go into row 14. Place your cursor in the cell that relates to column E on row 14.and click to highlight it. The cursor has changed to a cross. This cell is called **E14**.

You need to add up from row3-row 13 in column E. Go to the formula bar (white box at the top). The box on the left will tell you that you are in cell **E14**. Click on the white box on the right and type the following formula: =SUM (E3:E13) and either press '**Enter**' (↵) or left click on the mouse. The total £211.20 goes into cell E14.

You can also highlight the whole column and use the Auto sum function on the top right of the Menu Bar but it is important that you know how to do simple calculations using formulae.

The sum appears to work backwards. Firstly, it adds up the column using the information inside the brackets to get a total. I added up Columns F and G in the same way. To check that the total 'Cost incl. VAT' in G14 is correct, click on an empty cell and add E14 and F14 using the formula above. The result should be the same. Whichever cell you highlight with your cursor—that is where the result will be put. You may need to delete this final check, as it is not relevant to the record.

I actually found a mistake when I was setting up this spreadsheet, as I hadn't put a total cost in cell G8. **Crosschecking is essential. The figure in the final total box in the last column should be the same as the two columns added together.

You will notice in the screenshot [Fig 14] that the cursor has been placed over cell G14 in column '**Total of cost incl. VAT**' and the mouse left-clicked. The formula that added up cells G3 to G13 shows in the formula bar at the top of the page. The column is also showing plain numbers with one decimal place. That would need to be changed to make it consistent with the others.

	A	B	C	D	E	F	G	H	I	J	K
1	Jan-12										
2	Date	Description	Supplier	Number	Cost Ex Vat	VAT 20%	Cost Incl.VAT				
3	3rd	Stationery	J.Paper		£50.00	£10.00	60				
4	3rd	Pipes	A.Waste	3	£30.00	£6.00	36				
5	4th	Stationery	J.Paper		£30.00	£6.00	36				
6	5th	Milk	J.O.Caff	3 litres	£4.50	£0.90	5.4				
7	6th	Cleaning Material	M.Mopp		£15.00	£3.00	18				
8	10th	Stationery	J.Paper		£10.00	£2.00	12				
9	10th	Tea	J.O.Caff	Box 160	£3.50	£0.70	4.2				
10	11th	Gloves	P.P.Elf	5 pair	£25.00	£5.00	30				
11	23rd	Stationery	J.Paper		£30.00	£6.00	36				
12	23rd	Milk	J.O.Caff	4 litres	£6.00	£1.20	7.2				
13	30th	Postage	Post Office	20 2nd class	£7.20	£0.00	7.2	Postage is not VAT rated.			
14	Total				£211.20	£40.80	252				

The formula bar shows: =SUM(G3:G13)

[Fig 14]

Fig.14 is shown in what we call **'page break view'**. Menu Bar/View/Page Break View.

This shows that the page is in portrait i.e. vertical and that there are two pages. (If there was more information, the screen would be filled with more 'pages'.) The dotted blue line shows that the pages are broken in the middle of the table before the totals column. This is not really, what we want. We want to try and get the whole table on the same sheet (if possible).

There is a way to do this:

1) The table is a small simple one and there is some text to include on row 13 which makes it quite wide so we could change the orientation to 'landscape' or 'horizontal'. (Menu Bar/Page Layout/Orientation/Landscape.)

2) Move the mouse cursor over the blue dotted lines. The cross will change to a two-ended arrow. Left click and drag the lines to the end of the column you want to. In this case column J, so that we include 'Postage is not VAT rated' and all the table is on one page. [Fig 15]

	A	B	C	D	E	F	G	H	I	J
1	Jan-12									
2	Date	Description	Supplier	Number	Cost Ex Vat	VAT 20%	Cost Incl.VAT			
3	3rd	Stationery	J.Paper		£50.00	£10.00	60			
4	3rd	Pipes	A.Waste	3	£30.00	£6.00	36			
5	4th	Stationery	J.Paper		£30.00	£6.00	36			
6	5th	Milk	J.O.Caff	3 litres	£4.50	£0.90	5.4			
7	6th	Cleaning Materia	M.Mopp		£15.00	£3.00	18			
8	10th	Stationery	J.Paper		£10.00	£2.00	12			
9	10th	Tea	J.O.Caff	Box 160	£3.50	£0.70	4.2			
10	11th	Gloves	P.P.Elf	5 pair	£25.00	£5.00	30			
11	23rd	Stationery	J.Paper		£30.00	£6.00	36			
12	23rd	Milk	J.O.Caff	4 litres	£6.00	£1.20	7.2			
13	30th	Postage	Post Office	20 2nd class	£7.20	£0.00	7.2	Postage is not VAT rated.		
14	Total				£211.20	£40.80	252			

[Fig 15]

To go back to 'Normal View', in the View Menu box, click on 'Normal'.

As I explained earlier, when you open up the Excel Workbook it shows up as Book 1. If you haven't already done so, save it now. Go to the **'Office Button' on top left of the window /Save As (or File /Save As). Save it as 'Supplies 2012' and put it in a folder in the My Documents folder where you can find it easily. This record or workbook will cover each month for 2012 on a separate sheet that you can give a different colour. Have fun!

Headers and footers are added by going to the 'Insert' tab on the menu bar and following the options it gives.

This is just a very basic introduction to the basics of Excel to help you to become more familiar with what you may be expected to be able to do in a job, even if you will not be setting up the information. Being familiar with the software will help if you have to read and use information already input by someone else.

**If you would like to know more, another way of increasing your ICT skills in this and other topics covered in this chapter is to take your European Computer Driving Licence qualification that can be done online with one-to-one tutor support at http://www.ecdluk.co.uk/

Health, Safety and Security relating to ICT.

Everyone has a duty of care to others.

'In addition, the Health and Safety at Work Act 1974 requires employers and employees to take reasonable care for the health and safety of everyone at work, including visitors and other non-employees who use the premises.'

(Source:.http://www.worksmart.org.uk/rights/i_have_heard_about_a_duty_of 07.03.2012)

Six European Union Directives (known as the 'six pack' came into force in 1993 and were embedded in the Health and Safety at Work Act 1974:

1. The Management of Health and Safety at Work Regulations 1992—(more commonly known as the Management Regulations).

2. Workplace (Health, Safety, and Welfare) Regulations 1992.

3. Display Screen Equipment Regulations 1992 (amended 2002).

4. Provision and Use of Work Equipment Regulations 1992 (amended 1998).

5. Personal Protective Equipment at Work Regulations 1992.

6. Manual Handling Operations 1992.

You have the right to be protected when using a computer and an organisation must comply with the law in making sure that electrical equipment is safe.

However, you *also* have responsibilities as an employee and must not do anything, which could endanger yourself or others. Although health, safety and security in the workplace is covered in *Skills for Employability Part Two: Moving into Employment,* you do need to be aware of some of the important aspects of health, safety and security when using computers in the workplace or indeed anywhere. The next section of this chapter deals with that and some basic 'good housekeeping'.

The workstation or desk.

➢ Make sure that the wires are not a tangled mess. It is easy to have a heavy cable resting on a much lighter one but this can cause something to disconnect. Try to have all the cables free from each other. Do not wrap them over each other as this can break the finer wires inside.

➢ Slips, trips, and falls are the biggest cause of time off work. Make sure that there are no trailing wires over which other people could trip. Keep wires away from main traffic areas. If that is impossible, they should be taped down or enclosed in a special cover.

➢ Take regular breaks away from the screen if your work involves mainly computer work. This could be planned into your schedule as part of the day's work.

➢ Adjust your screen. There should be an eye distance of 50cm-90cm.

➢ Adjust your seat to the right height for you so that you are not straining with a viewing angle of about 20°; adjust the backrest.

➢

Task: ✐

Take a look at the website below for more details on how to avoid strain and what kind of chair you should be using. Your chair is actually a work tool.

http://www.healthandsafety.co.uk/CHOOSING%20THE%20RIGHT%20CHAIR.pdf

- Do not have drinks near the keyboard or your work. A simple accident can cause the loss of information on the PC, or on paper based copies of the information.
- Clear all rubbish from the desk into the waste bin.
- Make sure that the desk, computer, printer, and other equipment are kept clean.

A dirty screen means that you have to strain to see properly. A dirty keyboard and computer means that dust can get inside and could cause a malfunction. Apart from anything else, it doesn't give a good impression to either other people you work with or visitors. If you take care of your working environment, customers and colleagues can see that you will take care of them and your work. The office of a small works e.g. an engineering works, by its location in a partitioned area off the shop floor soon gets dusty. Do not be shy of picking up a cloth and dusting the screen, desk, and computer. You will be showing that you care and have standards, which will reflect on your work.

The manufacturer's instructions for cleaning and maintenance should be followed.

More information at http://www.hse.gov.uk *and*
http://www.pcs.org.uk/en/resources/health_and_safety/he
alth_and_safety_legal_summaries/display_screen_equipm
ent_regulations.cfm

Data Protection.

You have a right to know what information is being held about you and how it is being used. You also have responsibilities in relation to data protection; what information you can and cannot give out and who has the authority to have that information.

The Data Protection Act 1998 lays down the rules for dealing with personal and sensitive information—both paper and computerised. Individuals are allowed by law to find out what information is held about them by organisations who, by law, have to follow the eight principles of good information handling.

'The act contains eight 'Data Protection Principles'. These specify that personal data must be:

1. *Processed fairly and lawfully.*

2. *Obtained for specified and lawful purposes.*

3. *Adequate, relevant and not excessive.*

4. *Accurate and up to date.*

5. *Not kept any longer than necessary.*

6. *Processed in accordance with the 'data subject's' (the individual's) rights.*

7. *Securely kept.*

8. *Not transferred to any other country without adequate protection in situ.'*

(Source http://dataprotectionact.org/1.html 07.03.2012)

The 'Data Controller' in an organisation is responsible for making sure that the organisation complies with the act.

How does this affect me as an employee?

The bottom line for you as an employee is that you have to make sure that you keep information, paper-based or computerised, safe and secure and not give out personal or sensitive information to anyone who does not have the authority to have it. Just because someone asks for information, does not mean that they are entitled to have it.

The easy solution is to ask someone in authority if you are not sure.

The computer screen should not be in a position where anyone passing, and who should not have access to the information, can see the information on the screen. This includes visitors. Privacy screens are available.

One word of caution. Having jumped through all the hoops of searching for a job, sending your CV, going for interview etc you will be excited at having landed a job. It is tempting to chat away to friends in the pub or club or wherever it is that you socialise.

Remember! Loose talk = Lose business!

You never know who is listening or what the person you are talking to—even a friend—will do with the information, so one good rule of thumb is quite simple. Do not talk in detail about what you do or what your organisation does.

Go to the Information Commissioner's Office website: http://www.ico.gov.uk/ for more information.

Much of this *should* be covered at your induction but it is never too early to be aware of your responsibilities as an employee.

Copyright.

It is easy to search for images on the Internet and download them to your computer. But, beware! Before you use them, check that the pictures are not copyrighted.

You must have the owner's permission to use copyrighted work. If you look at the front of this book, there is a statement about the author's copyright. Copyright [written, theatrical, music or artistic work] lasts for the life of the creator plus seventy years from the end of the year of the author's death. After this, the work comes into what is known as 'the public domain'.

The UK and many other countries have signed up to the Berne Convention—the Universal Copyright Convention—which came into force in 1952 and amended in 1971. This means that these countries do not have to sign up for copyright protection as it is automatic.

'The law of copyright and its related rights in the UK can be found in the copyright sections of the Copyright Designs and Patents Act 1988 (as amended).'

More information at: http://www.ipo.gov.uk/types/copy/c-about.htm

In this chapter, we have touched on sending and receiving e-mails, using the Internet, record-keeping using Excel spreadsheets, and health, safety and security when using computers. This chapter, together with the knowledge you have gained in Chapters One to Three has set the scene for moving into employment.

'Where do I go from here?' you may be asking.

Take a moment to check your knowledge overleaf before moving on to the last short chapter—Progression.

Check your knowledge.

Put the answer below without looking back on the chapter.

1. Why is it advisable to organise e-mails into folders?

2. How do you do a search for a product or information on the web?

3. Why is it important to have cables tidied away?

4. Why is it important not to gossip about your organisation and work?

5. Who can you give personal/sensitive information to?

6. Who owns the copyright to written material?

Signposting to QCF.

Relationship of this chapter to the knowledge and understanding of other qualifications.

SSA 14.1 Foundations for Learning and Life.

14.2 Preparation for Work.

C&G Award and Certificate in Employability and Personal Development 7546.

> ➤ Introduction to ICT.
> ➤ Self-Assessment.

OCR Employability Skills.

> ➤ Preparing information effectively.
> ➤ Carrying out and learning from practical tasks.
> ➤ Learning about workplace values and practices.

Functional Skills. English. ICT.

> ➤ Reading.
> ➤ Use ICT systems.
> ➤ Finding and selecting information.
> ➤ Developing, preparing, and communicating information.

Essential Skills Wales. Communication. Use ICT systems.

> ➤ . Reading.
> ➤ Use ICT systems.
> ➤ Find, select, and exchange information.
> ➤ Develop and present information.

Progression. Where do I go from here?

After reading and completing *Skills for Employability Part One: Pre-Employment* you are ready find information that will help you once you have 'got that job'.

Skills for Employability Part Two: Moving into Employment will help you here. It is in the same non-threatening, user-friendly format, with space to complete a few tasks.

Forewarned is forearmed as they say so grab a copy (release date November 2012) and prepare for life in the workplace.

Depending on 'where you are at' in the scheme of things, you may be ready to think a little more about what you want to do and what your goals are. When you left school, you most likely would have been given a Record of Achievement folder with evidence of your courses and exams. It doesn't end here. You must keep up a record of what you have done both in work and in private life. Remember! No learning is ever wasted so record it all—formal, and informal through activities.

Many employers now are asking for some evidence that you have taken control of your learning and development, not only for your future success but also for that of the organisation. *Release Your Potential: Making Sense of Personal and Professional Development* takes the mystery out of this process and helps you to focus on your goals in life.

Contact your local Job Centre or college to find out about more training opportunities in your area or a new one.

Follow the links in the next section for more information.

Useful Links and Resources

http://www.apprenticeships.org.uk/Be-An-Apprentice.aspx

http://www.direct.gov.uk/en/Employment/Jobseekers/Loo
kingForWork/

http://www.direct.gov.uk/en/Employment/Jobseekers/Hel
papplyingforajob/DG_173785

http://wales.gov.uk/topics/educationandskills/learningprov
iders/essentialskillswales/

http://www.totaljobs.com/Content/Jobseeking_plus/Job-
centres.html

http://www.apprenticeships.org.uk/Be-An-Apprentice/The-
Basics.aspx

http://www.totaljobs.com/careers-advice/cvs-and-
applications/personal-statement and look at the examples.

http://www.totaljobs.com/Contents/cvchecker.aspx

http://en.wikipedia.org/wiki/Communication

http://www.hse.gov.uk/pubns/ppeindex.htm

http://www.worksmart.org.uk/rights/i_have_heard_about
_a_duty_of 07.03.2012

http://www.ecdluk.co.uk

http://www.healthandsafety.co.uk/CHOOSING%20THE%2
0RIGHT%20CHAIR.pdf

http://www.ico.gov.uk/

http://www.ipo.gov.uk/c-about.htm

http://windows.microsoft.com/en-US/windows-vista/Parts-of-a-computer

http://www.amazon.co.uk/Thank-You-Your-Application-ebook/dp/B007WRN2C2/ref=sr_1_3?s=books&ie=UTF8&qid=1335445564&sr=1-3

Further Reading

Lifelong Learning: Personal Effectiveness Guides.

Initially, the series will look at the background to lifelong learning and some research into various viewpoints.

Following this, will be an introduction on how to structure and develop your continuing personal development records. The basic principles here can be applied to any level in various degrees of complexity and are suitable for a cross-section of ages and occupations.

The series continues with the skills needed for employability and are in two parts.

Who are these books for?

> ➢ Aimed at the home learner and designed to read in bite-sized chunks.
> ➢ Someone who is unable to attend formal courses.
> ➢ To fill gaps in underpinning knowledge and skills needed to 'get on in life'.
> ➢ Designed as a user-friendly support material for learners of all ages with a wide range of abilities.

Lifelong Learning: A View from the Coal Face.

ISBN 978-1-908302-04-5. Also in e-book formats for most e-readers.

This is the first of the new Lifelong Learning: Personal Effectiveness Guides by Rosalie Marsh, which draw from her extensive skills & industrial experience in sales management and work-based learning in adult and further education.

This springboard for this new series of Lifelong Learning: Personal Effectiveness Guides revisits earlier research carried out which examined:

- ➤ Lifelong learning.
- ➤ Its meaning.
- ➤ The governments of the day's perspective and aspirations for the future.
- ➤ The experiences of a cross-section of professionals and educators when they were at school.
- ➤ The effects of the educational policies of the day on their progress then and that of their employees.

The research is brought up-to-date with a reflection of 'where we are now' and reference to the Wolf Report. It brings a new perspective and focus to this very relevant issue today.

The author looks at the wider issues of:

- ➤ Learning.
- ➤ Opportunity.
- ➤ Access.
- ➤ Professional and Personal Development
  before asking if the success of the initiatives is being effectively measured.

The results of the semi-structured interviews with a cross-section of mature adults had surprising results.

Release Your Potential: Making Sense of Personal and Professional Development.

ISBN 978-1-908302-08-3. Also in e-book formats for most e-readers.

This is the second of the new Lifelong Learning: Personal Effectiveness Guides by Rosalie Marsh, which draw from her extensive skills & industrial experience in sales management and work-based learning in adult and further education.

You are having a career change; you are looking to get into employment; you are looking to simply become more effective in your present role but don't know how to go about improving your skills.

If this sounds familiar—

Release Your Potential will help you to:

> ➢ Identify what you know now and need to know in order to improve.
> ➢ Look at how you learn best.
> ➢ Make best use of your time.
> ➢ Handle stress.
> ➢ Plan how you will achieve your goals.
> ➢ Develop and maintain a Personal Development Portfolio.

Skills for Employability.

Further titles in the new Lifelong Learning: Personal Effectiveness Guides by Rosalie Marsh, which draw from her extensive skills & industrial experience in sales management and work-based learning in adult and further education. It is a step in the personal and professional development journey where development of the whole person is at the heart of Rosalie's ethos.

In two parts, *Skills for Employability*—designed to be read in bite-sized chunks—will focus on some of the skills you need in order to impress an employer, stand out from the rest, become employed, and enhance your future.

Part One looks at the pre-employment skills needed.

ISBN 978-1-908302-16-8. Also in e-book formats for most e-readers.

Part Two looks at what you need to know when you move into employment.

ISBN 978-1-908302-20-5. Also in e-book formats for most e-readers.

Each chapter details the learning outcomes and relevance to other qualifications such as Personal Life Skills, Employability Skills, and Functional Skills. Through short practical activities, the learner will be able to see how far you have 'travelled' in gaining knowledge and understanding.

Skills for Employability Part One: Pre-Employment looks at those skills for the future, which include:

- ➢ Preparing for work.
- ➢ Job applications and a successful interview.
- ➢ Working effectively in the workplace.
- ➢ ICT skills in the workplace.

Skills for Employability Part Two: Moving into Employment looks at the standards of behaviour and requirements of employers:

- ➤ Introduction to health and safety in the workplace and Employment Rights and Responsibilities (ERR).
- ➤ The business environment and good working relationships.
- ➤ The importance of good customer service.
- ➤ Important aspects of managing your money.
- ➤ Progression. 'Where do I go from here?'

Some of the benefits of *Skills for Employability*.

- ➤ User-friendly. Can work at your own pace.
- ➤ Raised self-esteem and confidence.
- ➤ An increased awareness of the standards of behaviour and requirements of employers.
- ➤ An awareness and understanding of the business environment.

Who are these books for?

- ➤ School leavers; 16-18 yr old unemployed; returners to work; learners seeking a change of employment, wishing to enhance their prospects or, are between jobs.
- ➤ Aimed at the home learner and someone who is unable to attend formal courses.
- ➤ To fill gaps in underpinning knowledge and skills needed to 'get on in life'.

Just Us Two Travel Series.

During their first Gold Wing experience, finding that the words flowed when recounting their profound emotional experiences, Rosalie realised that there was the beginnings of a story. As the years passed, they extended their horizons, travelling over 50,000 miles on their own. Rosalie wrote about their amazing experiences as feature articles, eventually concluding that together they formed an inspiring story of adventure and realisation of dreams. Rosalie wanted to share their story and so, with the support of 'Ned', *her* baby was born.

Just Us Two: Ned and Rosie's Gold Wing Discovery.

ISBN 978-1-908302-12-0. Also in e-book formats for most e-readers.
Winner 2010 International Book Awards (Travel: Recreational).

Finalist 2009 Best Books Awards (Travel: Recreational). USA Book News.

Just Us Two is an exhilarating romp through ten happy years of discovery, adventure, and fun! Ned, in middle age wanted a little bike to tinker with. Rosie discovered a majestic Gold Wing motorbike and swopped well-groomed hair and high heels for a crash helmet and biker's boots. Share their thrills and spills as they discover long lost family in Ireland before jaunting around Europe to follow Rosie's dreams . . . travelling on their own—*Just Us Two*.

What readers say about Just Us Two.

'Inspiration for us all to motorcycle touring overseas.'
Editor Motorbike Search Engine.
http://motorbike-search-engine.co.uk/motorcycle-product-reviews.php.

'Not just for bikers!'

'Rosalie's passion for travel, adventure, and living life to the full comes across so beautifully in her narrative and her book *Just Us Two* which I highly recommend. Rosalie's thirst for knowledge and personal development has driven her to write and share her wonderful experiences – a true inspiration to me and I believe to anyone who aspires to live life without 'if onlys'.'
Chrisoula Sirigou, ExploramaEU.

'The descriptions . . . so wonderful I felt I was there, on the motorbike.' Jean Mead. Author.

'A gifted author who can bring her travels books alive. She has a wonderful sense of the ridiculous and her style as a raconteur means that the reader feels she is talking personally.' Judith Sharman. Well-Tree-Learning.

'A great read that will make you smile.' Editor, Trike Magazine.

Read the sequel *Chasing Rainbows: with Just Us Two.* The second in the Just Us Two series and the real ending to Rosie's Gold Wing story.

Chasing Rainbows: with Just Us Two.

ISBN 978-1-908302-00-7. Also in e-book formats for most e-readers.
Sat Navs! Do you love them or hate them?

Chasing Rainbows is the real ending to Rosie's Gold Wing story. Now, no longer able to ride, this intrepid couple finally say good-bye their Gold Wing motorbiking days but only after more adventures; this time not on a Honda Gold Wing'; this time not quite Just Us Two . . .

In this new saga, a hidden controller, in the shape of disembodied voice with which Rosie conducts a 'love-hate' relationship as it threatened to make her navigating skills redundant and ruin their next big trip, accompanies them.

Now, 'Ned' has come out of the shadows and reverted to his given name, which is how he appears in this light-hearted and often tongue in cheek story of discovery and adventures. He also has a new toy. You know boys and their toys. It is infallible; trusty will lead them to wherever they want to go. No stress; no trouble; no getting lost . . .

Take in the beauty of Ireland and Co.Mayo; the breathtaking wonder of the Andorran mountains; the awesome grandeur of the Spanish Pyrenees; Visit Versailles and Paris as Rosie chases her rainbows . . .

What readers say about Chasing Rainbows.

'Another great book by Rosalie Marsh that should not be missed. The flow of words employed to narrate it, is in itself most refreshing.' Joseph Abela, Author, on Chasing Rainbows.

'A great follow up to *Just Us Two*.' Amazon reader, on Chasing Rainbows.

Rosalie Marsh titles are available worldwide in print and e-book formats for most readers.

Christal Publishing

www.christalpublishing.com

Lightning Source UK Ltd.
Milton Keynes UK
UKOW030757170513

210838UK00002B/101/P